THE SINGING VOICE

Thank you to every student who has ever spent an hour with me. Between us, we've nutted this much out.

The Singing Voice

AN OWNER'S MANUAL

For Singers, Actors, Dancers and Musicians

Pat Wilson

Illustrated by
George Aldridge

CURRENCY PRESS • SYDNEY

NICK HERN BOOKS • LONDON

First published in 1997 jointly by
Currency Press
PO Box 2287
Strawberry Hills NSW 2012, Australia
and
Nick Hern Books
14 Larden Street
London W3 7ST, United Kingdom

Revised reprint 2001
Copyright © Pat Wilson, 1997, 2001

NATIONAL LIBRARY OF AUSTRALIA CIP DATA
Wilson, Pat, 1943–.
        The singing voice.
        Bibliography
        Includes index
        ISBN 0 86819 494 8 (Currency Press)
        1. Singing 2. Voice – Care and hygiene. I. Title
783.04

A CIP catalogue record for this book is available from the British Library,
London
ISBN 1 85459 382 X (Nick Hern Books)

Cover designed by Anaconda Graphic Design/Trevor Hood
The mouth design at the beginning of each chapter by Kirsten Faith
Typeset by Currency Press
Printed by Southwood Press, Marrickville, NSW

ACKNOWLEDGEMENTS FOR REPRODUCION OF LYRICS
Page 13 'Wherever He Ain't': Reproduced by permission of Warner/Chappell
Music Australia Pty Ltd. Unauthorised reproduction is illegal.
Page 20 'A Quiet Thing': Reproduced by permission of Warner/Chappell
Music Australia Pty Ltd. Unauthorised reproduction is illegal.
Page 29 'On My Own': Music by Claude-Michel Schonberg. Lyrics by Herbert
Kretzmer.
Original text by Alain Boublil and Jean-Marc Natel. © Copyright (music and
lyrics) 1980 Editions Musicales Alain Boublil English lyrics © Copyright 1985
Alain Boublil Music Limited. This arrangement © Copyright Alain Boublil
Music Limited. Used by permission of Music Sales Limited. All rights reserved.
International Copyright Secured.

Contents

Acknowledgements

I would like to thank the following people for their help in the preparation of this book: Adrian Barnes; Chris Backhouse; Dr Donald K. Bartram, BDS, BAc; Dean Carey; Robert Gammal BDS; Robin Gist (especially for Chapter 12); Jeannie Hurrell (especially for Chapter 11); Isobel Kirk; Chrissie Koltai; Dr David Mitchell, MB, BS, FAMAS; Chris Morley (especially for the Appendix); Aarne Neeme; John O'May; Noël C. Tovey; Miguel Trapaga; Jack Webster; Anthony A. Williams.

Praise and thanks alike are due to my editor, Dawn Titmus. I am very grateful for the helpfulness of the staff of Currency Press, in particular the unfailingly kind and wise Julia Collingwood.

I would especially like to thank George Aldridge for his wonderful illustrations and Kirsten Faith for her wonderful mouth at the beginning of each chapter.

If Len Sandery hadn't been the singer, the teacher and the father that he was then this book could never have been written. He taught me the joy of singing and encouraged me to sing my joy.

If the late Sandra Gorman hadn't been such a clear-headed, plain-speaking, loyal and trustworthy friend then this book could not have appeared in its present form.

Foreword

After reading Pat Wilson's *The Singing Voice — An Owner's Manual* I felt I had spent time with a good friend who knew her facts and knew how to help me. All performers must strive to present themselves at their best — this is all very well but we are human and our insecurities and weaknesses often get in the way. Pat acknowledges this with a common-sense, no-nonsense approach, a wealth of solutions, sound advice and a good sense of humour.

The modern music theatre requires us to stretch our range and register to accommodate scores with highly dramatic themes, and those productions also need the stamina and technique to maintain our well being for very long seasons. Many of the ideas, exercises, maintenance programmes, health tips and remedies are new to me and I look forward to embracing them. This book is a 'must have' for anyone who aspires to a career in the entertainment industry and for experienced performers who wish to be stimulated, enlightened and reminded that you can never stop learning.

Nancye Hayes

Introduction

This book is for people who have already done some singing training. It is not a how-to-sing manual, but is aimed at people who want to keep their voice in good shape.

If you fondly recall all that voice work you did with your last singing teacher, or at drama school, at university or at the conservatorium, and if you often think, 'I ought to keep my voice in trim', this book is written for you.

This book will help you to maintain your skills. It will remind you of your industry's requirements, and give you some hints and short-cuts.

Landing a job on the strength of your voice is one of the most exciting things that can happen to you. Empty-handed, we singers create magic from breath, bone and tissue alone.

So here's to us: royalty amongst musicians, the only ones to play our music upon an instrument not made by human hands.

Every instrument is unique and irreplaceable. When its player dies, the instrument dies too.

We who take on the world of music in unarmed combat should remind ourselves now and again of the sheer alchemy of our trade. Vocal wizards — here's to us!

CHAPTER 1

Overture

*Song is the breaking free of the soul, the impetuous headlong expression
of the joys of life.*
Epitaph of British actor Sir Laurence Olivier

This is a resource book of practical hints, advice and information for trained performers who need to keep their singing voice in working trim, whether they work in opera, theatre, musicals, modern dance, rock or jazz bands, or as session singers in sound studios.

THIS IS NOT A HOW-TO-SING BOOK

I believe that the best way to learn to sing is with the encouragement, support and instant feedback of another person as instructor. Hence, this is not a how-to-sing book.

I presume that you have been taught how to sing or that you are currently studying singing. Perhaps you went to a conservatorium and graduated with a major in singing. Perhaps you trained as an actor, where attention is always given to your singing as well as your spoken voice. Good dance-training courses often include singing training, as many modern-dance choreographers are now demanding sung and spoken voice skills of their dancers. In addition, there are more employment opportunities available to trained dancers who can at least booth-sing (adding one's voice to the on-stage sound by singing into microphones in an off-stage booth) when not on stage in a musical. Maybe you are working one-on-one with a singing teacher. Whoever you are, if you're a performer, you're likely to need your voice.

WHAT? NO STERNOCLEIDOMASTOIDEUS?

Because I presume that you have already studied singing, I have not included helpful anatomical diagrams showing side views of the human head with cut-aways to demonstrate the location of your vocal cords and associated apparatus. Nor have I included any recommended vocal exercises or vocalises. You have your favourites, built into the technique you now use.

WHO ARE YOU?

You're probably a trained actor, dancer, musician or singer. You have learned singing as part of your professional training. Quite probably you have a weekly lesson with your singing teacher or vocal coach in order to maintain your skills, broaden your range and diversify your repertoire. You are now working, or auditioning for work, in opera, theatre, musicals, modern dance, rock or jazz bands or for session singing in sound studios.

Once you have been employed to perform, and that performance includes singing, you will find yourself faced with a barrage of questions, many of which may not have been considered during your training. Topics such as finding repertoire, dealing with accompanists, choosing the best microphone, keeping yourself in performance trim, understanding industry expectations and anticipating the rigours of touring may not have been taught exhaustively at your school or conservatorium. It is these kinds of practical considerations that this book addresses.

REPERTOIRE

Faced with a shop full of sheet music, how do you pick out a song that you love? And even if you love the song, how can you be sure that it will work well as a performance piece for you? Will you be able to wrap your voice around it, or is it a bit too difficult for you to attempt at this stage? Does it offer interesting acting possibilities while showing off your voice to best advantage?

LEARNING TRICKS

Once you've selected a song, I can offer some suggestions to help you to learn songs quickly and competently. You may need to be reminded that singing lyrics demands an actor's skill; it's wise not to take your actor's hat off once you burst into song on stage. Where your body is and what it does are also as much a part of your singing performance as the sounds that come out of your mouth.

CLEAR SOUND

If you are to serve with integrity both your audience and your text, you will find it useful to consider some technical questions concerning the clarity of the sound you make. The chapter on vowels and consonants will probably recall some of the things your voice teacher or vocal coach used to teach.

TERROR

Stagefright can be a real hurdle to potentially brilliant performers. It has halted many careers. All of the practical advice in the chapter which discusses fear is based on either my experience or that of friends and colleagues in the profession.

THE ACCOMPANIST IS NOT THE ENEMY

If singers do not understand what an accompanist does, and if they do not know how to work with an accompanist, they are likely to make horrible blunders. The fact that these sins are committed in ignorance makes them no less embarrassing. I can speak feelingly about both sides of this area, since I also work as a professional accompanist. What accompanists can do for you and what you should do for them, together with the general etiquette of working with accompanists, are covered in Chapter 8.

AN AUDITION IS A JOB INTERVIEW

Because of the peculiarities of our industry, performers will find themselves applying for jobs far more frequently than workers in other professions. Our job interviews are called auditions, and the skill of audition is a special one which is allied to, but somewhat different from, that of performance. In an audition, there are niceties to be observed and pitfalls for the wise to avoid. In this chapter, you will find everything you always wanted to know about auditions ... from the most simple practical tips to a philosophic analysis of the audition process.

GOING COMMERCIAL

Once you have been hired to do a production, your employer will immediately have a range of professional expectations of you as a worker, firstly in rehearsal, and then in the run of the show. Understanding trade practices for artists will give you confidence as you enter into employment. Whether you have been hired by the management of a musical show, a country tour of a theatre-in-education piece, a rock group or an opera company, most of the principles are the same.

POPULAR MUSIC

Here's a term that always makes me flinch. It seems to imply that any music which doesn't fall into this category is automatically classified as unpopular. Tough luck, Mozart.

Semantics to one side, it seems to me that many otherwise splendid performance training institutions still neglect this area. I hope this oversight is not evidence of a residue of old-fashioned cultural snobbery. The pop and rock music scene is as legitimate a professional performance area as, say, opera or music theatre. It sometimes pays better than both of them put together, and it has its own industry codes of conduct. Speaking from an entirely technical viewpoint, you will need to build roughly the same order of vocal stamina should you seek a professional career in either opera or heavy metal music.

SINGING IN A STUDIO

Even seasoned live performers can feel daunted when faced with the alien culture of the recording studio. Its impressive paraphernalia can hamper a singer's style; seemingly distanced from their flesh-and-blood audience, some singers clam up and deliver emotion-free sound.

Knowing what you are likely to face in a recording studio should help you to modify your artistic approach in order to work happily within this vital medium. I know how handy it is to face studio sessions armed with a few practical hints about headphones and microphones, and some basic information covering the social conventions and technical expectations of sound recording work.

TAKE CARE OF YOURSELF

Lifestyle issues are of paramount importance to actors, dancers and singers, because their means of earning a living are entirely body based. Every singer knows you can't pop down the shop and buy a better instrument. Nor can you book your instrument in at a good technician's workshop for a clean and overhaul of the action. Instrument maintenance is a daily do-it-yourself process for singers.

For this reason, I have included information on health and fitness. When you have to be able to deliver a quality performance no matter what, it's useful to have a resource list of recommended medical and complementary holistic therapies.

There are activities you can undertake which are positively beneficial for vocal performance. Some elements of environment and diet can assist your voice, while others may have the opposite effect. There are numerous simple and practical ways to structure your lifestyle in order to enhance your vocal work.

All singers dread catching a cold. But when a cold threatens, there are useful strategies you can use to help you keep going, build up your immune system and help minimise adverse effects of the infection.

The special needs of the many performers who are prone to asthma are covered in a separate chapter, which has been co-written with Dr David Mitchell.

The Bottom Line

In today's cost-sensitive world, producers habitually moan about their financial constraints. They will tell you (at length) how they suffer from working within an industry which has an indecently sporadic cash flow. Next thing you know, they've transmitted some of their tension to the performers they hire.

If you're not quick to learn, apt to take direction, confident, pleasant to work with and utterly reliable (in attendance, general health and vocal quality), management will swiftly remind you that there's a queue of fine performers out there who are all of the above and would love to take over your job, thank you.

I'll have to leave the 'quick to learn, apt to take direction' areas up to you. In this book, you should be able to find sufficient essential, practical and current information about both the performance industry and vocal craft to ensure that you are confident, pleasant to work with and utterly reliable.

CHAPTER 2

How to Pick a Song

I used to while away the hours memorising recipes from Fine French Cookery. Sometimes I'd play my banjo. Once, I sang the recipe to borscht à la russe en gelée to the tune of 'Click Go the Shears', and it worked out really good. The chorus was always the list of ingredients, and the verses were the directions. It worked out so well I was soon singing filets de sole bonne femme to the tune of 'The Man from Snowy River'; pintades roties to 'Waltzing Matilda'; and selle d'agneau jardinière to 'Lulu's Back in Town'.

Mandy Sayer, *The Cross*,
Angus & Robertson, Sydney, 1995

As a performer, you will find yourself spending a huge amount of time rehearsing and performing material you have not chosen. Once cast in a show, you do what the book and the score demand, whether you are charmed by it or not.

When it comes to choosing songs to add to your repertoire for audition or concert performance, give yourself the chance to display your vocal range, your acting skills and your musicianship. Pick songs you enjoy, with music you love and words which don't make you wince when you read them aloud.

If you are working on audition songs, make sure they can be cut down to run for no longer than two minutes, without sacrificing either musical or intellectual content.

THE COMPONENTS

Songs comprise three elements: *music*, *words* and *meaning*. Yes, words and meaning are different. You realise this when you hear a person with a glorious voice singing a song's lyrics clearly and carefully, but with no idea of what the song's about. They'll smile endearingly while singing of death and distress. Or the song's all about their new lover, but they might as well be singing about fish fingers or reinforced concrete. At times like this, I don't believe the old song when it says 'Two out of three ain't bad' ... A singer needs to address all three elements of a song.

When you get the chance to pick your own songs, select material that's strong in all three areas.

MUSIC

When you choose a song to perform, bear in mind that you want to show off your musicianship to its best advantage. Also remember that music is not all sound — it is silence too.

> **Music is the presence and absence of sound.**

Flatter Your Voice

Pick a song that's got some musical complexity in it; one that not everyone could handle. An interesting and unpredictable key-change, a hard-to-sustain soft but high passage, long notes that you can hang onto better than others. By now you know the strongest bits of your vocal technique. Pick a song that displays your strengths and shows the least of your weaknesses.

Be careful to avoid songs with a huge range if your own vocal range is fairly limited. I am not referring here to songs that are written in keys too high or low for your voice: this problem is easily rectified by transposing the music. For instance, if the piece you want to perform is written in too high a key for you, transposition will lower the whole song; you'll start on a lower note and the highest note in the melody will be just that much lower too. (Of course, the lowest note of the melody will also be that much lower.)

If, however, your current vocal range is one-and-a-half octaves, it is simply practical for you to avoid two-octave-range songs, no matter how much you love them. Consider them as incentives for you to keep working at the breadth of your range by consistent vocal exercise under the guidance of your singing teacher.

The Presence and Absence of Sound

Music is both the presence and absence of sound. When you think of music, think of lace; the holes are as important as the threads. The pleasing patterns made by the threads wouldn't be there if it weren't for the holes. It would only be a tea towel or a hanky, instead of a doily. The pauses in music, the rests, the breaks from unrelenting sound — these are as large a part of your musicianship as the glorious sounds that fall from your lips. As you choose music and then devise your artistic approach to the work, always remember the pivotal importance of the *absence* of sound. This fact holds just as true for Mozart as Metallica.

WORDS

Show off your appreciation for finely crafted lyrics. Words that speak directly to you when you read them as text; words that have an elegance about them, that feel right when nestling within the music they're written for; words you wouldn't feel stupid saying out loud without the benefit of the music.

Unspeakable Lyrics?

A good way to test the quality of lyrics is to imagine yourself walking into a local shop and just *saying* the words of the song out loud — for instance, to a shop assistant — as dialogue.

> **We sing when emotions become too intense for mere speaking.**

Off the top of my head, I can list a good number of lyrics I'd feel stupid saying out loud. One easy example is the lyrics of 'Feelings' (originally 'Dime?') by Albert/Fundora. I can't see myself standing in the deli saying, 'Feelings, wo wo wo, feelings, wo wo wo, feel you again in my arms'. I find these lyrics unspeakable.

Even though the words of some songs may make sense, the lyric writing can sometimes feel inexplicably lumpy and at odds with the music. Avoid these songs, even if you can't quite work out why you feel that way about them. Trust your bones as a performer.

MEANING

Show off your skill as an actor. Pick a song that has a story, so you can have the fun of telling it in as engaging a way as possible. Many songs with wonderful music and carefully crafted lyrics have no journey within them: they state one thing and then restate it, and then, in case you hadn't noticed, they say the blessed thing all over again. A good song should be a three minute opera, with a beginning, a middle and an end. Its plot must so intrigue me that I can hardly wait to hear how it all turns out.

The Song as Journey

In this area, you pick a song in much the same way that you'd pick a monologue for an audition. You are ill advised to do a speech that starts with vehement bellowing, keeps at it for two and a half minutes and ends with more of the same. No journey of the spirit, no highs and lows. Just a good test for the vital capacity of your lungs and the good nature of the audition panel.

It is equally counter-productive to pick a wistful, wispy, half-whispered piece of dreamy monologue — when that's all there is to it.

Select a song which will take your listeners on a trip. Find one whose opening words deceive, cajole, tease, amaze, arrest or terrify. Let them do *anything* but be safe and predictable. If we all know how it's going to turn out, what's the point of the story? Where's the suspense?

This criterion of a song's worth works perfectly well even if the song is a well-known one. Just as an old fairystory told night after night still holds the power to amaze and delight when recounted by a fine story-teller, a familiar song may still be thick with undischarged tensions, even though we know it from way back, when it's in the hands of a good actor/singer.

Appropriateness

There are many songs which you could probably sing very capably but which are totally inappropriate for you. Do not be tempted to perform them, however much you love the pieces. Your age, skin colour, build, gender and ethnicity all combine to present a picture of you. If your appearance is at odds with the message of the song, you risk looking silly and you will unwittingly amuse rather than entertain.

If your audience is laughing for quite the wrong reasons, you have lost it; the beauty of the music and the value of the lyrics are forgotten while it laughs at a 45-year-old man singing 'Sixteen Going on Seventeen' (*The Sound of Music*). Or imagine a 16-year-old girl attempting to make dramatic sense of 'Wherever he ain't' (*Mack and Mabel*). No matter how good a singer she is, her task is made impossible by her appearance. An unfit and unco-ordinated singer attempting 'Hey, Big Spender' stretches our willingness to believe and improves her chance for failure. Can a short, stocky, lethargic man tackle 'Sweet transvestite' (*Rocky Horror Show*)? One hopes that he doesn't try it; the result is too ludicrous to contemplate.

It is here that you need to pause and discover the story of every song. Chapter 3, 'How to Learn a Song', and Chapter 4, 'Acting as a Singer', will help you to choose songs appropriate to your persona and career.

Choice of a song is a lot like choosing clothes that minimise your figure faults and emphasise the very best bits of your body. This may sound obvious, but anyone who regularly auditions performers will tell you that a lot of people are fatally attracted to the wrong song for them.

WHAT'S IT FOR?

Are you trying to pick the ideal song to audition for a music-theatre production? It's unwise to do a song from the show unless you are specifically asked to do so. Why? The audition panel may have set ideas about how it wants this song performed. *See* Chapter 9, 'The Art of the Audition'.

Are you looking for a song to perform with an originals band? Always ask the band what its major influences are, and try to do material that it's likely to enjoy and make sense of. Showing off your vocal ability in a musical form that the band members are unlikely to appreciate, let alone require, is a waste of time. If it's a reggae band, forget Mahler and try Marley.

Is it a covers band? Obviously, you should polish up a range of material that fits in with the band's areas of musical interest.

A tribute band? Even easier: it wants a Beatles look-alike and sound-alike; you turn up looking like a Beatle, sounding like a Beatle and singing a range of Beatles repertoire. This is the only circumstance where accurate mimicry of the record will land you the job.

Even though your best showpiece is Cole Porter's magnificent 'Love for Sale', dig out another song when a Christian TV program wants to hear your work.

When you're up for the job of presenter on a children's television show, 'Hey, Big Spender' isn't your best bet as an audition song.

You're auditioning to get into a training institution? Try to avoid songs like 'Nothing' from *A Chorus Line*. Why? It's too long, it's self-indulgent and downbeat when done outside the context of the show, and it's done to death by a zillion aspirant performers. For similar reasons, that lovely introspective song from *Fame*, 'Out Here on My Own', is equally inadvisable.

You get the idea: exercising intelligent choice is a matter of old-fashioned common sense.

CHAPTER 3

How to Learn a Song

*When with your mind you free your ear
and take the dancing words inside
they'll occupy such certain space
accordant with your hearing then
you'll give the song its round and end,
from tongue to page and back to tongue
to utter with your voice my song.*

Kevin Pearson, 'Songs IV' in *No. 4 Friendly Street Poetry Reader*,
Friendly Street Collective, Adelaide, 1980

The most effective approach I have found in preparing for the performance of new material involves a sequential formula: it starts with paper,
proceeds to the words of the song and then to the music.

Like most formulas, if you skip a step, do it in a different order or substitute
ingredients, you run the risk of not achieving a perfect result. Learning a new
song will involve you physically, emotionally and intellectually, as you
memorise and then make sense of its three component parts — music, words
and meaning.

PAPER

First, always work from printed (or composer's manuscript)
vocal score if at all possible. Here's the essence of the
composer's intentions and an accurate rendering of the
lyricist's text.

> **If the words don't matter, it's not a song.**

It is never advisable to work from lyrics which are, at best,
a set of educated guesses made as you replayed the CD or
tape into oblivion, trying to make out the words. Nor is it musically
respectable to offer your accompanist or band members a heap of scribbled
chord symbols which represent your best estimate of the music.

LEARNING THE WORDS

1. Write the lyrics out fully: no 'etcs', no 'repeat chorus', write every word you have to sing. Handwriting on ordinary, lined paper is probably the best way to do this.

   Don't write out the lyrics in one long block as if they were a letter:

   > Once a jolly swagman camped by a billabong under the shade of a coolabah tree, and he sang as he watched and waited 'till his billy boiled, you'll come a-Waltzing Matilda with me. Waltzing Matilda, Waltzing Matilda, you'll come ...

   A big slab of undifferentiated text is not memorable. Write your song out like a poem:

   > *Once a jolly swagman*
   > *Camped by a billabong*
   > *Under the shade of a*
   > *   coolabah tree*
   > *And he sang as he watched*
   > *And waited 'till his billy*
   > *   boiled*
   > *You'll come ...*

   It takes much more paper but less brain to remember the shape of the lyrics.

2. Now *say* it all out loud in a deadpan, non-rhythmic way. Don't try to sing the song, simply say it. And again. This process stops you from worrying about three things at once while you're learning lyrics. You don't have to think about *music* or *meaning*; you merely concern yourself with memorising what *words* are where.

   Trying to learn a song by singing along with a recorded performance of it introduces too many elements at once. It complicates your learning process and is also likely to inhibit your freedom to give the song your own unique interpretation.

   Soon you will have memorised the words. Making sense of them is the next process, one which you shouldn't start worrying about until you have memorised the text.

3. Once the lyrics are snared within your memory, you're in a good position to think about what they mean. Imagine telling someone the story of the

song. Use *none* of the key words but *all* of the sense of the song to convey its story to someone.

For instance, you've just memorised all the words to 'Wherever He Ain't':

INTRO
This ninny of a puppet was available the second
that he called.
And all he had to do was yell, 'Hey, Mabel!',
and this dumb hash-slinger crawled.
For seven lousy years
I've watched him swear and sob and shout.
With you or with out you?
Well, it's gonna be without.

SONG
I gotta give my life some sparkle and fizz
And think a thought that isn't wrapped up in his.
The place that I consider Paradise is
Wherever he ain't!
Wherever he ain't!

No more to wither when he's grouchy and gruff,
No more to listen to him bellow and bluff,
Tomorrow morning I'll be struttin' my stuff
Wherever he ain't!
Wherever he ain't!

Enough of being bullied and bossed.
Ta-ta, auf wiedersehen, and get lost!

I walked behind him like a meek little lamb,
And had my fill of his not giving a damn.
I'll go to Sydney or Ceylon or Siam;
Wherever he ain't!
Wherever he ain't!

(Original lyrics © 1974 Jerry Herman, from the show *Mack and Mabel*.)

Using the rich resources of these vigorous and colourful words, you'd probably tell your imaginary friend something like:

INTRO
This little twit of a ventriloquist's dummy made herself
available whenever he demanded it.
All he did was yell for me, and I'd turn up: much like
a menial waitress.
I've listened to him whinge and bellow for years on end.
Now I've got to decide whether I'll keep putting up with

his carryings-on or not.
I've made up my mind — no, I won't.

SONG
I need to give my life some pizzazz.
I need to think independently,
For me, the best spot I can think of to be at the moment
is wherever he doesn't happen to be.

I will take no more of his grumbling.
I will take no more of his yelling.
Early on the morrow I'll be showing myself off
as a pretty neat proposition — in whatever place
he doesn't happen to be.

I am tired of his overbearing treatment of me.
I'm telling him — Good-bye; get stuffed.

I felt imprisoned by our relationship;
I became weary of his carelessness.
I now will happily travel very far away
in order to be in a place where he isn't.
(and so on ...)

There's another verse or so to go, but you get the idea of the meticulous thoroughness with which you need to approach this work. Turn the meaning of the song into a lively, well-expressed story that you're confident of telling. Make sure all the nuances of the text are securely in place.

Now you can start thinking like an actor about the performance of the song. Text merits close attention, and all the clues for your acting decisions are contained firstly, within the words, and secondly, within the music.

Once you have identified the ideas within a song, you can make intelligent choices about performing it — not before.

LEARNING THE MUSIC

Can you read music? Can you sight-sing? Do you play a musical instrument? If you have even one of these skills, you're well on your way to learning the music independently and with confidence. If you intend earning your living by working with music every now and then, you should at least learn to decode musical symbols so they make sense to you. It is never difficult to find a cheap beginners' music theory night class; they are frequently on offer through local adult education outlets. Teach-yourself books are also a low-cost, effective means of learning basic principles of the symbology of music.

Although there will be times when there is simply no other way, playing the album again and again and singing along with it is never the ideal way to learn new material. For all the reasons listed in Chapter 4, this is a limiting and second-best way to learn a song.

Furthermore, if you have found it impossible to locate the score for the piece you want to do, your accompanist is stuck with listening to the tape repeatedly, making notes and then attempting to transcribe the piece for playing. This is a process frequently attended by panic; most accompanists will do almost anything to avoid having to work this way.

> Every song is a three-minute opera: it has a beginning, a middle and an end. Its plot must so intrigue me that I can hardly wait to hear how it all turns out.

The best ways to learn the music, in order of preference, are:

1. *Work the song out for yourself* by reading the score. You could either sight-sing it if you're a fluent sight-reading singer, or play the vocal line on a piano or whatever melodic instrument you can manage. You do not need to be much of a musician to do this. Even if you read music dreadfully slowly and have scant instrumental skill, working systematically through the vocal line is still your best means of making sense of the music of a song.

2. *Get a musician to make a learning tape* for you. Pianists/keyboardists are likely to be of the most use to you for this sort of learning process. Give them a copy of the score and ask them to play onto a cassette tape *just the melody* you have to sing. Request a very strict rhythm, and get them to do it at a slower pace than the performance speed of the piece (unless it's a dirge). A good idea is for them to play your single line of notes accompanied by a metronome set at a speed that you both agree is a good learning pace.

This tape will give you a clear line of exactly what is written in the score, for you to learn and sing. This is not karaoke. It will have none of the seductive qualities of a 'sing-along-for-the-fun-of-it' tape. It's sternly exact — no more, no less.

When the melody-only track has been done, ask your musician to do a recording of the accompaniment of the song, played at your preferred performance pace. This will give you a sing-along version; it offers you an opportunity to check how thoroughly you have learned the melody. Ideally, the musician will hardly play your melody line at all in this track; they'll leave it entirely to you, playing only what the accompaniment indicates.

When you can't read music and have no skill in any musical instrument other than your voice, you're somewhat at the mercy of others' kindnesses. You need that melody track to be entirely accurate. If you intend doing an improvisational jazz version of a song, you may never end up singing each note as it is written and played, but you *must* know the basic song thoroughly before you can take liberties with the written melody.

Bluesman John Hobson has an apt aphorism for this: you have to be fluent in a language before you can swear effectively in it. This is exactly the degree of easy familiarity you need to have with a song before you can perform it, let alone improvise upon it.

CHAPTER 4

Acting as a Singer

Listen to me, watch me, don't decide what you're going to do until you see what I have done. Come on, Tristan — you want to act. This is acting — the moment while you wait to hear what I say. While you think what to do — that's it. It isn't the lines, or the lights — this is what we give them: the energy, made by this gap which is made by you listening to me. Drama is a spark plug. Your listening is the gap, the spark flies across.

(Peter Carey, *The Unusual Life of Tristan Smith*,
UQP, Brisbane, 1994.)

Every song has a beginning, a middle and an end. It has a story; a plot which should engage my liveliest curiosity, tug at my emotions and have me intrigued, wondering 'What will happen next? How's it going to finish?'

As story-teller, it's your job to make me believe that story and care about its outcome. All those words transmit meanings, frequently at more than one level, and their significance will demand all your acting skills to interpret the lyric as a piece of spoken dramatic monologue.

Performers who stop acting as soon as they start singing devalue both arts. The same factors which inform an actor's intelligent and emotionally truthful presentation of spoken text hold equally true of text that is sung.

Text drives emotion. *Emotion* drives performance. If words didn't matter, a song would become an instrumental. You could whistle it or play it on a guitar and it would be just as effective. If the words don't matter, it's not a song.

LOVE THAT LYRIC

An actor may or may not sing; a singer must always be an actor. Despite such exceptions as scat singing in jazz, and 'Bachianas Brasileiras No. 5; Aria: Cantilena' by Villa-Lobos, when words have been deliberately set to the music, one gets the idea that the composer and lyricist intend a direct acting transaction to be made using their artwork: *Here's my story — you tell it.*

Music alone contains meanings and emotions. Well performed, it will convey much from both the composer's and the interpretative performer's spirit. When music has words fitted to it, your job as a singer is clear: to communicate as best you can those nuances of both story and music which have been entrusted to you. It's a sort of contract. When you undertake to learn and then perform a song, it's as if you have entered into a solemn agreement with its composer and lyricist to free the essential meanings you discover encoded within the net of words and music. In this way, your audience may see, hear and feel all that the song's originators ever intended — and even more than this.

> **An actor may or may not sing. A singer must always be an actor.**

Here's where your own creativity comes in; as an artist, you also have the right and the obligation to place your own interpretation on the raw material of the song. A singer must always be an actor, a chameleon of the soul.

THE SIN OF THE SING-ALONG

Interpretation is a matter of leaving your fingerprint on a song. All performers have a uniqueness which makes their performance entirely distinct. Unless you're headed for a gig with a tribute band, never, ever try to do a song exactly the way you've heard it recorded. Even if it's your top favourite CD or tape or video — especially if it's your top favourite.

If you phrase every bit of the song exactly the way Barbra Streisand does, if you hang on to that note as long as she does and use that cute little run-up to the middle eight, just the way she does on the record — *Bad news!* You'll still never sound like her, so why try? *Good news!* She'll never sound like you, either, so your career path's clear — you can get out there and be a gloriously unique, incomparable, distinctive, individual performer.

There are even more disadvantages to learning a song by singing along with the recording. It is difficult to listen critically to your own voice when you're buoyed up on a continual ocean of luxurious sound. 'Ooh, it sounds so great when I sing along with Domingo; and I know I could do it just as well as he does, if only I had a decent orchestra like that behind me.' Really? How would you sound in a practice room accompanied on piano by a good repetiteur?

If you know the song — really know the heart and mind of the song — then you can sing it convincingly and well without singing along with your *Music Minus One* tape using 70 per cent echo on your mike. We're not talking about fond dreams now: if you want to work as a voice professional, you need to free your own voice and then listen intently to it.

Singing along with the recorded version teaches you to phrase the song in the ways that the record's performer has chosen. This automatically cuts you off from thinking about how *you* want to go about structuring your performance, and about how *you* want to interpret the text and the music. There you are, singing along and absorbing that glossy, seductive, finished product by whom? Te Kanawa? Streisand? Farnham? Patinkin? Bortoli? Sting? Whoever they are, they'll have spent a long time generating their very own theatre of performance on this song; and oops! you've swallowed it whole, without thinking. When you get around to performing the piece yourself, you'll find you're regurgitating whole chunks of *their* reading of the song — unquestioned, unexamined and therefore not from your heart or mind. This matters, because your performance is bound to be two-dimensional at best. Copying a song from a recording is like living all your life in someone else's shoes.

'UP' SONGS/'DOWN' SONGS

Sometimes you'll pick a song that's perfect for your voice and equally perfect for your purpose, then quite promptly 'go off' the whole idea. This happens frequently with some performers, especially the anxiety prone.

It is most likely to occur when the song you've chosen is slow or sad or quiet, or a combination thereof. You'll mumble to yourself 'This is so bland. It's too slow. It's such a 'down' song. What can I make of it? I don't want to depress my audience; I want to engage, delight, arouse and excite it. Quick — let's find something bright.'

And so you risk making a beginner's blunder: confusing entertainment with brisk pace and cheerfulness. You want to choose something that you think your audience will readily enjoy; one that will make it like you. As a result, you find yourself always picking happy songs or fast songs, or sometimes both.

An unrelenting diet of lollipops is boring. Many auditions request preparation of two contrasting songs, so you have the chance to show your versatility. Every well-planned program contains contrast and variation. Diamonds display best on a bed of black velvet.

Develop a director's eye for a good, slow song. Does it have a vicious undertow in the text? An unexpectedly humorous quirk in the coda? An insistent funereal rhythm that you can use to enhance its presentation? Bring your actor's cunning to bear upon fine songs which deserve your careful consideration and artistic production.

Have you got a song in mind which you love dearly but fear may be too bland? Is it all pale beige to you from top to bottom? Try to find within it each of the stages of grieving as enumerated by Elizabeth Kübler Ross and then reflect these emotional levels in your interpretation of the song. Where's the anger? The blaming? The resignation? The denial? This exercise cannot help but develop your actor's imagination and sensitivity, as well as assist your growth in stature as a performer. As a bonus, your repertoire improves.

AN ACTOR SINGS

Yes, you love the music. Perhaps your favourite recording star wrote and performed it. You're keen to perform it. And now, a three-step acting task can make this song yours.

Learn it

Perhaps you might like to try the formula to learn a song presented in Chapter 3. However you go about it, do make sure that you have learned the song thoroughly. Don't attempt step 2 until you've fixed step 1.

Find a character

Having mastered the basics, you've had time to think about what the lyrics say and how the music supports them. Your next job is to work out *who* is singing the song. This person doesn't need to be the same sex, age or nationality as you. If the song comes from a musical show, you don't need to be limited in your thinking by the character who sang it in the show. Neither do you need to know the show, nor the song's place within the plot.

You will need only two sources from which to fabricate this character: your lyric and your imagination. Ask yourself, for instance:

- How old is this person?
- Where do they live?
- In what era do they live?
- How do they earn their money?
- What's their name?
- What's their greatest fear?
- What sort of shoes are they wearing?

In addition, you will need to have two pictures in your mind to help your character come to life. These scenarios will act as the framework of the song's action.

Picture #1: A snapshot of what happened just before the song started that caused your character to feel the way they do and gave them the need to tell us about it in the song.

Picture #2: A snapshot of what is going to happen to your character and the world around them as soon as the song finishes. How does the song change their universe? What is the resultant action?

Once you've answered all these questions and feel comfortable with your discoveries, here's a useful second-level analysis question: You've won a cruise for two to Fiji for three weeks. Would you ask this character to accompany you? This is a good way of checking how lively and valid your character is, as well as finding out whether you actually like the character or not. You don't have to: some of the best creations you may ever come up with may be the most hateful of human scum; folk with whom you wouldn't share a rancid

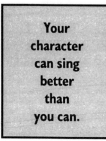

Your character can sing better than you can.

cheese sandwich. It's a pity that some singers are slow to confess how much they hate the character who has emerged from their investigations; they somehow think that they ought to love all their protagonists.

Let's be grateful that the horror and crime novelists don't feel squeamish about creating monsters for us to revel in when we read. Give me some monstrous characters in your singing and you'll gain and keep my interest too. Dean Carey, author of *The Actor's Audition Manual*, observes 'You may not like [the character], but you must understand their motives and empathise with them, or else you'll comment on the character and play negative judgements'.

As an example of finding a character to sing a song for you, let's use the lyrics of 'A Quiet Thing' from *Flora, the Red Menace* by John Kander and Fred Ebb:

When it all comes true
Just the way you planned,
It's funny, but the bells don't ring.
It's a quiet thing.
When you hold the world
In your trembling hand,
You'd think you'd hear a choir sing.
It's a quiet thing.

There are no exploding fireworks,
Where's the roaring of the crowds?
Maybe it's the strange new atmosphere,
'Way up here among the clouds.

But I don't hear the drums,
I don't hear the band,
The sounds I'm told such moments bring.
Happiness comes in on tip-toe.
Well, what-d'-ya know!
It's a quiet thing,
A very quiet thing.

(Original lyrics © 1965 Fred Ebb)

Careful analysis of the text plus your actor's imagination could yield any number of characters to sing this very gentle, lovely song. Here's one option; it's what I imagine when I sing it:

My name's Laura; I'm 38 years old, and I have a Master's degree in pharmacology. My specialisation is in viral strains. I live on my own and am not currently in a relationship. I'm tall but fairly solidly built. Wavy, brown hair. Softly spoken. Don't care much about fashion. I have parents who were born in southern Italy and wanted all of their children to make something of themselves when they came to Australia. I was born in Australia, but although I honestly feel more Australian than Italian, I respect old ways too.

Mamma has repeatedly begged me to get married, have kids, settle down, but I'm so focussed right now on the importance of my work that almost anything else feels secondary to me — especially since I've been working in virology.

It's late at night in a multistorey building which houses administrative offices and research laboratories for the pharmaceutical company I work for. I'm on my own in the laboratory I share with my fellow scientists. I've stayed back because I thought there was something odd in the results I got from the batch of tests I ran just before I was due to leave work at 5 pm.

As the song begins, I've just put my clipboard down by my computer terminal on the lab bench, and sagged wearily onto the nearest backless stool. It's 3 o'clock in the morning, and I have finished every possible cross-test on the effectiveness of a chemical compound that I just had a mad hunch might be the answer to a killer virus which has begun wiping out newborn children in large hospitals worldwide. I've found the one thing which can safely bring this rogue virus to a halt, without inflicting any harm on the delicate metabolism of a baby.

I'm bone-weary and the small of my back aches constantly. I've been on my feet for hours; luckily, I always wear jogging shoes in the lab. But as I think of the immediate possibilities of this cure in the fight against this virus, I marvel that here, in the still night, with only the hum of computer monitor and air-conditioning to stir the silent air, so momentous a secret has popped open before me. It's so important! It will be a worldwide life-saver, a major international medical breakthrough. And there's no-one but me that knows this silent secret yet. For all my weariness, I feel like shouting. There should be a big brass band, banners, all the pomp of a parade.

I sit slumped on that hard metal stool, and I sing — to myself — to marvel at the wonder of the moment.

When the song finishes, I smile to myself, stand, stretching slowly. I lock away the clipboard in the bottom drawer of my desk, scribble a note to the head of research saying I'll be in late for work tomorrow, close down my terminal, pick up my briefcase, turn out the lights, walk to the lift, the front doors, the car park

and then drive slowly home in the silent streets of the night city.
My heart is strangely calm and joyous.

You will no doubt find a totally different character and scenario from these lyrics; that's the joy of an actor's approach to a song. The lyrics could as easily support these possibilities:

- You are a mountaineer who has finally made it to the top of a mountain peak. Immense cost and years of planning culminate in silent, solitary exultation at the summit of the mountain.
- You are a woman who has just given birth; finally left alone to rest and recover by staff and attendants, you are physically exhausted but emotionally elated.
- A person whom you have admired from a distance has just confessed to you that they love you and hope you love them. And you certainly do.

In imaginative work of this kind, the whole creative rainbow of dramatic possibilities lies before you. If your character and scenario choices are supported by the text and fit well within the style and feel of the music, then they're right for you.

Let your character sing the song for you

There is a golden rule, invariable and simple: your character can sing better than you can.

Your created character will have none of the embarrassment, shyness or intellectual reservations that you may have about the song. Their commitment is total and their energy is awesome because of the completeness of their belief in those words and what they stand for.

Your character will always sing the song better than you can — so why don't you be silent and let them get on with it!

CHAPTER 5

Dancing as a Singer

*She dances as if she does not know any one is there. Her expression is
one of concentration and her whole body belongs in the fantastic rhythm.
The uneven hem of her dress has seductive qualities.*

Elizabeth Jolley, *Miss Peabody's Inheritance,*
UQP, Brisbane, 1983.

I f the basis of music is the presence and absence of sound, then the basis of
dance could be said to be the presence and absence of movement.

Know where your body is — it matters. It's worth remembering that your
face is part of your body; it's the prime visual site for your audience to derive
clues about your performance. Body awareness is important for all singing
performers, even those intent upon building a career out of voice-overs and
studio recordings.

Your body's positions and movements tell a story just as clearly as do the
lyrics of a song or its music. Think how useful it can be: you've got another
dimension with which to communicate. Let your face and body help interpret
the story.

Although the above may sound obvious, there is plenty of evidence that it
needs to be said out loud quite frequently to many performers.

TRADITION AND STYLE

The dead weight of tradition is exactly that. Don't let the traditional
limitations of your area of performance art weigh you down. Why strap a dead
elephant to your head?

There are *usual* approaches and presentation behaviours associated with
every genre of performance. Unthinking acceptance of 'what they usually do'
can ensnare otherwise perceptive singers. Be wary of the traps.

Just because recital artists seem compelled to stand in the well of a grand
piano and impersonate an ironing board with eyebrows, there's no need for
you to swell their ranks.

Just because jazz singers seem to treat their mike stands like walking frames, and limit their body movements to finger snaps and only such stylised hip swings as are approved by unspoken agreement within jazz cadres, why should you?

Just because lead singers in rock seem to frown, stroke their mike and adopt a standard, high-stepping, jiggly jog reminiscent of leaping in and out of treacle, who says you have to?

Just because performers in musicals always seem to sing with a manic, wide-eyed grin and do embarrassingly cute arm and hand gestures, there's no need for you to copy them.

EVERY TIME YOU SING, YOU HAVE TO DANCE

Every area of sung performance, with the exception of recordings, demands performance information from your face and body. Yes, every time you sing, you have to dance. Of course, this doesn't mean that you're obliged to jump up and down whenever you sing. I mean that your body's stance and movements bear constant, corroborative witness to the information of your performance; you should be wholly aware of where your body is and what it's busy telling your audience.

Your body dances all the time, whether you're conscious of it or not, whether you'd call it a dance or not. Even if your body conveys information about the song you are performing by its absolute stillness, this, too, is a discipline of motion, a dance. And dance conveys an instantly assimilable sequence of information. Best that it works *for* you rather than *against* you.

When you sing, where are your hands? Across the front of your body all the time? Perhaps protectively clasped over your groin area? Plucking at the side seam of your pants? Grasping the mike stand as if you're about to drown?

Do you move from side to side with the rhythm? What does it look like? Do you shift from one foot to the other? Do you attempt to gesture, feeling that you want to free your arms, give them something to do? Do you look like a seagull when you do all that stuff?

Perhaps you have a series of postural habits which you have unconsciously absorbed from your training in classical singing. Be aware of these, and examine their appropriateness in the light of the material you are preparing for performance.

What is your face doing as all that glorious sound pours out towards your audience? Do your eyebrows do a manic twitch as you negotiate more complex melodic patterns? Do you perform a sad song with a nasty grin on your face, in a desperate attempt to 'place' your sound by a sort of smiling technique? It will give your poor audience all the wrong emotional cues. As a rule, it's best to try not to use too many of the external muscles of the face to form your sung sound. When singers do this, they often look as if they have far too much chewing gum in their mouths and they're trying to sing around it. The effect varies from unfortunate to comical.

Internal muscles of the face and throat can help you to sing; then you can use your face to act with — it's a great help towards the believability of your performance. *Your best singing happens when you use your speaking face to sing with.*

As an actor (and *all* singers need to be actors), you know how you feel about the song you are performing. You should understand the emotions you wish to communicate to your audience. Are your face and body part of all that, or are they working against your every intention as an actor?

COGNITIVE DISSONANCE

As an easy and educational field-study project, try to spot the 'schizoid' singers whenever you watch sung performances. These are singers whose bodies betray what their lyrics would have you believe. Sometimes, even while their faces are entirely engaged in a fine acting performance, their stance and movement are so inappropriate as to be ludicrous. Singing one story with your words whilst expressing an entirely different one with your body can frequently provoke unintended mirth in one's audience. 'Schizoid' performers can often teach you a great deal, especially in the 'what not to do' category.

> **Use your speaking face to sing with.**

Watch a singer laying a steamy love song out before an audience; the words ensnare, the music seduces, the singer's face reflects erotic promise. But the singer's body looks like a dead fish, or it twitches desultorily in a sort of auto-pilot disco manner.

Or observe a man with a big, broad, testosterone-soaked voice who, with out-thrust chin, sings of rough, tough, manly stuff. He stands slumped on one hip with the other leg angled forward, in time-honoured drag-queen pose, and rubs his left hand nervously up and down the side seam of his trousers.

I still recall a memorable audition performance where 'Feed the Birds', that innocent and sweetly plaintive song from *Mary Poppins*, was sung beautifully by an enthusiastic candidate; her every movement and gesture were pure striptease.

It will not take you long to collect a range of 'schizoid' performance favourites of your own.

If the visual impact of your performance contradicts the sound you produce, you will create cognitive dissonance. This disadvantages both you and your song. When you perform, you simultaneously relay both visual cues and verbal messages to your audience. If these two kinds of information are at odds with each other, you will confuse your audience and undermine the impact of your story.

All you really need to do, in order to work in harmony with your text and your acting choice, is to be aware of your body and be conscious of making it available to express your character. Usually, this will ensure that your visual presentation is integrated with your character.

CHAPTER 6

Vowels and Consonants

*Edwards, the music student, suggested a negro spiritual, and they began
to sing "Swing low, sweet chariot". The battery of voices in that confined
space, all trained to hit a note so that it went down and stayed down,
was terrific. Phryne felt tears prick her eyes, as she joined in, and
Marion was openly snuffling.*

Kerry Greenwood, *Murder on the Ballarat Train*,
Penguin/McPhee Gribble, Melbourne, 1991.

You hit your thumb with a hammer. You cut yourself accidentally. In shocked surprise, what's the first thing you utter? It's unlikely to be, 'Dear me, that hurts'. My prediction is that you'll say any one of a horde of single vowels or diphthongs. Try 'OWW'. Or 'AOW'. Perhaps 'OOOO'.

If you're terrified, you might scream. You may go 'EEEEE'. Or 'AAAAA'. Listen to the lines the film's scriptwriter gives to the person pushed off the top of a tall building or over the edge of a towering cliff. There he goes — 'EEEEOOOO AAAAAA!'

Vowels give us the most immediate, plangent snapshots of the heart. They get to the meat of every emotional matter. It is the vowels of a language which transmit the emotions: they are the revelation of the raw soul.

It is because of this that vowels form the heart of whatever song you sing. Honour them, learn to enjoy them and recognise your dependence upon them — for without vowels, we cannot sing.

YOU CAN'T SING A CONSONANT

The vowel is the singer's friend; the consonant is the singer's sworn foe. You can't sing consonants. Try singing 'n' — you sound like a door buzzer or an electric toothbrush. How about 't'? — you find you have to sing something like 'ter' in order to make a sung sound instead of just spitting.

Can you sing 'w'? It becomes, in desperation, 'wuh'. Attempt a 'v' — at best, your lips will tingle and you will sound like a mosquito.

Try any consonant and the results are uniformly woeful. Although we have to live with them, the best we singers can hope for is an intelligently negotiated compromise with consonants, whatever the language we sing.

Consonants tend to inhibit sound; vowels enable singing.

THREE QUALITIES IN SUNG SOUND

There are three qualities of sound in all singing:

1 Your singing voice.
2 Silence.
3 The consonants.

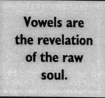

Vowels are the revelation of the raw soul.

The degree of artistic judgement which you exercise over qualities 1 and 2 will determine the level of excellence in your performance. *But* how much of the first two you are able to produce will be a function of the extent to which you can control the third of these elements. It is only by the careful management of these three components that you can build a mastery of sound.

Consonants have to be correct, clear and in the right place, but never more than you actually need in order to start the precious vowel or to finish it.

THE JOB OF A CONSONANT

Yes, they actually do something useful. A good consonant is much like a razor blade: very high-tensile steel but wafer-thin and flexible. Consonants act as de-limiters of vowels. They provide the start and the stop of the sound, and help to modify the vowel quality — nothing more.

THE PENCIL TEST

A good way to remind yourself of the primacy of vowels and the terrible tendency of consonants to gum up your singing is to subject yourself to the Pencil Test:

1 Take an ordinary pencil; *not* a propelling pencil, a ballpoint pen or a fountain pen as they tend to be too thick.
2 Place the pencil in your mouth sideways, holding it between your teeth.
3 Smile cheerfully.
4 Sing any song you've been working on, whilst holding the pencil between your teeth. (If you feel rather foolish, imagine you're a Carmen sort of character with a rose between your teeth.)
5 Every so often, remove the pencil in mid-phrase and listen to your voice.

If the quality of your sung sound changes markedly when you do this curious trick, it's quite probably because holding the pencil between your teeth enables the back of your throat to relax markedly, allowing more of your sound out.

Yes, some of your consonants will be hindered; don't worry about that. This is a test of the quality of your vowel sound. The Pencil Test helps to remind your body how best to get out of the way so your sound can fall out of the front of your face, unhampered by constraint of any kind.

Another useful rule of thumb is to look in a mirror while you're singing and check if you can see any of your teeth. If all you can see is a dark aperture framed by your lips, with not a flash of white, then you're probably singing in a vowel-obstructing way (or you've removed both your top and bottom dental plates).

What to Do with Consonants

Keep them in their place. Make sure they do their honest day's work but don't allow them to take over. When you think of consonants in a song, regard them as mint plants in your garden. You never plant mint directly into a garden: you plant it in a flower pot, so it can't take over the whole backyard.

Depart each vowel with affectionate reluctance; despatch each consonant with resentment. A consonant is like an olive pip.

Vowels in Text

As a practical exercise, look at the words of Eponine's song, 'On My Own' from *Les Misérables* (Kretzmer, Boublil and Schönberg).

> *On my own*
> *Pretending he's beside me*
> *All alone*
> *I walk with him till morning*

This is a slowish song (marking is Andante; crotchet = 72) which demands a sustained, legato technique. If you don't look out, you may find yourself singing

> On my ownnn
> Pretending he's beside me
> All alonnne
> I walk with him till morninnng

> **Depart each vowel with affectionate reluctance; despatch each consonant with resentment**

Your sound can easily become restricted by consonants, especially the sung 'n'; a noise which resembles an electric toothbrush.

There is an underlying principle which can assist singers, particularly singers of English, a language clogged with consonants. The idea is this: if you can transfer a consonant from the end of its syllable to the beginning of the syllable immediately following, you will be able to use your vowels.

Here's how you can apply this principle to the practical task of singing any text with clarity and freedom. The example above, when broken into syllables, looks like this:

On | my | own |
Pre- | -ten- | -ding | he's | be- | -side | me |
All | a- | -lone |
I | walk | with | him | till | mor- | -ning |

See how many syllables end with a consonant?

On / own / -ten- / -ding / he's /-side / all /
-lone / walk / with / him / till / mor- / -ning /

NOTE: '-lone' and '-side' end with consonants when you *say* them.

From a possible score of 20, there are 14 syllables which terminate in a consonant. In my experience, 70 per cent is a reasonable average for English-language lyrics.

Without technical analysis, most folk would sing this lyric word by word, just as they would speak it. This makes for a bumpy, disconnected sung sound, as the consonants keep switching off your opportunity to sing. This is the reason for using an open-ended syllable approach to the text.

Instead of articulating each word as an independent unit when you sing, try to end each syllable with a vowel. This enables you to hang onto the note written for that syllable for as long as the music indicates or for as long as you think you'd like to. Technically, this makes the above example look like:

O | nmy | o | wnPre | te | ndi | nghe | 'sbe | si | dme |
A | lla | lo | neI | wa | lkwi | thhi | mti | llmo | rni | ng.|

Although the lyric now resembles misspelled Welsh, try *saying* each of these syllables out loud, dragging out the vowels and minimising the time you spend on the consonants. Don't neglect any consonant, but don't hang onto them either. In this way, you can test the singability of the lyric without having to sing a melody as well. Next, sing the lyric in just the same manner. You should experience greater freedom from the tyranny of consonants.

Now you can see how the idea works, this deconstruction technique can be applied to any lyric where an accretion of consonants threatens to make the text difficult to sing.

THE OBLIVIOUS AMERICAN

No discussion of vowels for today's singers is complete without mention of a common flaw which appears too frequently in performers of all ages — the unconscious use of a sung American accent.

Thoughtless Americanisation of your singing is to be avoided at all costs. I have seen numberless pop and jazz singers and devotees of musicals transform from Jekyll to Hyde in an instant. If you ask them to *say* 'I'm gonna sit right down and write myself a letter', that's just what they say.

Asking them to *sing* the sentence results in: 'Arm gunna sid rye darn en ride mah se-af er leddah'. Why is this so?

If the character you are playing is American, then your accent is not only entirely defensible but also necessary. You have strong justification for your choice. In most cases, however, the Americanisation is simply a clear indication that the performer has given no thought at all to the character of the person singing the piece. It often indicates that they've studied a recording in order to learn the song, and they've taken no subsequent time to make the work their own by giving it an individual interpretation. People who sing Bette Midler's songs with exactly Bette Midler's phrasing, emphases and improvisational riffs are pathetically easy to pick. They also give fearfully boring performances.

> **You don't sing with your larynx; you sing with your heart and your head.**

The performer you are best able to present is you: work out what accent is right for the character (*see* Chapter 4, 'Acting as a Singer') and do it in that accent. Don't be seduced into the unstated belief that spoken information is readily received in your normal speaking voice, whatever your natural accent, but sung information can only be imparted in an American accent. Note: None of the above applies to Americans.

CHAPTER 7

Dealing with Fear

I shall not fear.
Fear is the mind killer.
Fear is the little-death that brings total obliteration.
I will face my fear.
I will permit it to pass over me and through me.
And when it has gone past I will turn the inner eye to see its path.
Where the fear has gone there will be nothing.
Only I will remain.

Bene Gesserit, 'Litany against Fear' in Frank Herbert, *Dune*,
Victor Gollancz, London, 1986.

Why do we fear? What causes it? Why should you be afraid? There are times when you ought to be terrified. You have every reason to fear if you have failed to prepare for your work.

If, for instance:

- You have not had a *sound check* in the venue with the sound rig in full working order.
- You have never worked on stage in the *costume* you're supposed to be wearing.
- You have never sung with your *accompanist* (or with the band) before the performance.
- You haven't *learned* the performance material as well as you possibly can.
- You haven't had a technical rehearsal to clarify what special *lighting* effects you need to know about (follow-spot? specials you need to hit at particular times? is the stage spiked for them?).
- You've been a genuine temperamental *brute* to the cast and crew of the show.

> **Sometimes there are fewer rules than you think.**

On occasions such as these, I wouldn't dream of saying 'Don't be scared' to you. As a performer, you deserve your terror.

However, despite careful preparation, serious application and a love of their craft, some performers are riddled with disabling fear before a performance. Fear inhibits auditions and diminishes performances. It has been the unspoken reason behind the quiet retirement of many wonderful performers. However strong you are, it is inevitable that you will run out of courage if a demon walks at your elbow every time you go on stage.

THE PHYSICS OF FEAR

The surface of tense muscle is porous, and absorbs sound. The surface of relaxed muscle is smooth, and enhances sound by bouncing it off its surface.

If you're busy producing sound in a cranny of your body which is surrounded by tense muscles, a good percentage of the sound you're making is being swallowed up by that porous muscle surface.

It's the difference between singing in a bathroom, with all that bright bouncy sound surrounding you, and singing in bed with the quilt and blankets pulled over your head and much of your sound absorbed by the bedclothes.

THE PSYCHOLOGY OF FEAR

If you hold fear in your neck, your voice is constantly flavoured with the fear it

has to travel through before it gets out to us. We, your audience, can smell that taint of fear. Even if you work like mad to conceal your terror, we can smell it.

You know how dogs can always sense people who are afraid of them? Audiences are much the same. It doesn't take experience or training for an audience member to smell terror on a performer. Audiences may not be able to analyse the cause, but their appreciation of the performance will have been marred.

THE PHYSIOLOGY OF FEAR

Muscles contract, movement is hampered. Breath becomes restricted. Blood vessels constrict; people become 'pale with fear'. Headaches develop.

The body loses moisture: the throat and mouth become dry. Fear creates excess perspiration, or the need to urinate or vomit.

None of the above is a great state in which to perform.

THE MYTHOLOGY OF FEAR

MYTH: If you're nervous before a performance, you're going to perform well. If you're relaxed and worry-free you're sure to turn in a less-than-brilliant performance.
REALITY: Come off it. (*See* above.)

'Ah', you say, 'but I read this article about [and here insert the name of a performance idol of yours] and it says that s/he is always terrified before they go on to perform. And that's what makes their work so magnificent.'

Your belief in the media is touching, if misplaced. When stars get asked yet another bunch of predictably fatuous questions, what can they tell the interviewer? The truth? 'I take my work seriously. I treat my performance as a task; a series of skills for which I'm paid rather well. If I fluffed around getting panicky every night, how could I ensure consistent excellence in my performances?'

It would make your average performer's attitude to work sound as glamorous and sexy as an engineer's. It's truthful. But it doesn't sell papers or boost the TV ratings.

Fear and Adrenalin

Don't forget that adrenalin is not fear. Anticipating performance will almost always produce adrenalin, but the performer may have no disabling fears relating to the coming event. The way your body prepares you for a challenge — even a pleasurable one — includes many of the symptoms which may remind you of fear. Adrenalin produces a heightened state of pre-performance anticipation, with extra energy provided through dilating blood vessels. Every performer learns to make good friends with adrenalin and to utilise the natural high; being laidback and nerve-free is an unusual state in which to approach performance. Few would recommend it as an ideal to work towards.

FIXING FEAR

There are a number of things which can help you if you are one of those unfortunate people who find themselves frozen with fear and incapable of performing. Attend to whatever you can, bearing in mind that this fear thing is a hurdle between you and the free mastery of your skills. You have undoubtedly conquered some hurdles already: problems such as a limitation in your vocal range, a nasty, ropy area in your transition between registers or some sort of vocal vice. You overcame those so you could go on to perform with greater effect and less hindrance. Treat this as just another one of those things to be fixed up. Enlist someone's aid and sort it out, so you can get on with the real stuff.

First Fix up what You Can Yourself

If your fear is mildly rational and stems from something that can be dealt with, try actually sorting it out instead of being a worry-wart. And if the task of speaking rationally about a rational fear seems too much for you at the time, enlist a friend to accompany you and help you to articulate the concerns you have.

If, for instance, a costume you have to wear in a show feels as if it is about to fall off during certain movements you have to make, talk to wardrobe and get it better structured to feel secure. If that worry inhibits your work, the company will suffer, so if you get no joy from a gentle word to wardrobe, perhaps you should chat to your company manager. It worries you? It slows down your performance, despite your best efforts? Then until your fears are allayed, the production suffers. Don't suffer silently and allow the fear to take a greater bite out of your mind. Your effectiveness will be further diminished.

You may have flying work to do in a harness. You may have seen the fly-man — the mechanist who rigs, tests, and flies your mechanism nightly — drinking significant amounts of liquid from containers that were unlikely to contain water. And you're pretty sure that the stage manager doesn't know about this. You may well be terrified. I think I would be. Some fear is well placed.

Some performers get a name in their trade for being whingers. They are querulous and dissatisfied, always grumbling and worrying. Of course, there are a whole host of ways in which you can make your fears known in order to sort them out. Because you are an actor (because every singer must be an actor; *see* Chapter 4), you will be able to broach your concerns tactfully, graciously and effectively, without becoming known as a grumbler.

A number of methods can be used to help allay fears (*see* Chapter 16 for further information):

Hypnotherapy

Qualified health care professionals offer this treatment, and it's often the treatment of choice for performance fears. A fair number of qualified hypnotherapists are also medical doctors. Some sage practitioners also have skill in other holistic therapies, too; it's doubly useful if you can find one of these.

Hypnotherapy will work for you if, despite the strength and ferocity of your fears, you truly wish to be rid of them. If you're using fear as a mask behind which you can shield your inadequacies, then hypnotherapy may not be able to help. Your fears protect you and, at this stage, you may need the safety and insulation of your fears more than you need to work.

Acupuncture

A non-invasive way to realign the internal balances within the body. If your fear flows from an out-of-kilter system, acupuncture may well help to restore neural and chemical equilibrium. Your fear responses may need to be unlearned after the physiological causes have been fixed up, but you're well on your way to complete recovery.

Bach Flower Remedies

Another fine naturopathic treatment, credited with frequent successes. Mimulus is the likeliest therapeutic agent. It is also worth remembering the range of curatives available in Australian bush flower remedies.

Homoeopathy

A dose of Argentum Nitreum taken before the performance, will frequently give remarkable results. However, it should not be taken continuously for more than five days; keep in contact with your homeopath if you use this remedy.

Psychological Counselling

An intelligent and perceptive psychologist may be just the right catalyst for you. Psychologists are not always mad-eyed behaviourists with a Freudian bent. Much like dentists, they've suffered as a profession from the comedy sketch brigade. Counselling sessions with a psychologist can be remarkably helpful, particularly for enabling you to view areas of your life in ways you may never have seen them before.

You will often find that you hold within you all the facts you need in order to overcome your fear. What is frequently lacking is a fresh point of view: that unique angle of perception which we sometimes find almost impossible to obtain from our own efforts. With a bit of a nudge from a person who is neither a working colleague nor family nor yet a friend, 'the penny drops' for many people. A new point of view gives new information, and you find that you no longer need your fear.

CHAPTER 8

Working with Accompanists

The piano is such a lonely instrument, she thought: always by yourself with your back to the world.

Helen Garner, *The Children's Bach*,
McPhee Gribble/Penguin, Melbourne, 1984.

When you sing a song, it's yours to present; the accompaniment is exactly that and no more. The tomato sauce isn't the pie; the mint sauce is not the roast lamb. It's the song that matters, and you own the song.

The singer must take responsibility for the performance of the song. What volume? What pace? What 'feel'? These are questions which only the singer can answer.

A good accompanist cannot be blamed if your song is too fast or too slow — accompanists must take their pace from you. If you hurry up, so will they. When you slow down, so will the accompanist. It therefore makes a lot of sense to get used to being the boss of a song: that is, not waiting for your musical accompaniment to jolly you along, but initiating all the moves yourself. You lead. This takes practice.

MUSICIANS OR ACCOMPANISTS

> **The singer owns the song.**

All accompanists are musicians, but not all musicians are accompanists. Because your friend got honours in grade 7 piano, and can rattle off a Beethoven sonata, don't put an Elton John song in front of her and expect her to accompany you faultlessly. Not even a Puccini aria. Why? Because you have both been trained to work as front-line soloists. Your pianist friend is used to having her own way, and so is a vocalist (unless you're in a choir or vocal group, or working as a backing singer).

An accompanist's unique art is their commitment to a mutually derived product which is managed by the soloist and facilitated by the accompanist within a symbiotic relationship.

YOUR SCORE

When you work with an accompanist, there are certain points of etiquette relating to the music score you bring along with you.

The Accompanist's Copy

Always bring a copy of your music for the accompanist. Don't turn up with your book, plonk it on the piano and sing cheerily over the poor accompanist's shoulder all afternoon. There are a number of good reasons for this:

- The accompanist will need their own copy on which they can feel free to note all the things they'll learn from working with you. They will want to scribble themselves little reminders all over the piece: slow down here, louder there, hang on to that note much longer than is written. Their art depends on shaping their music to fit your interpretation, so that together you present a seamless musical product. They can't scrawl all over your book, can they?
- When you've gone home, they'll need to practise the piece between now and whenever they work with you again. Just the same as you.
- Your voice mightn't be the nicest thing for them to have in their left ear for two hours. Ever heard of too much of a good thing?
- Do you have halitosis? Do you smoke?
- An accompanist follows *you*; your pace, your style. If you stand behind them, they can't see your breathing pattern, or watch your face to work out when you're about to start singing the next phrase. They need to *see* you all the time — that's part of their craft.
- Many people find it off-putting to have someone looking over their shoulder as they work.

Prepare the Score

Give the accompanist their own copy of your score as separate, photocopied sheets of paper sticky-taped together in a concertina fashion, thus:

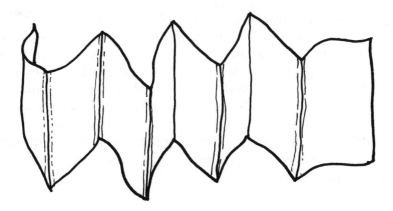

This either minimises or eliminates the problem of page-turning.

- Don't put sticky tape over any printed area of the score if you can help it. You try writing with a pencil on sticky tape. I personally prefer to stick the pages together by running masking tape vertically along the backs of the pages, using butt joints. Masking tape's low-tack adhesive is easy to work with, and it forms durable hinges.

- Make sure the photocopy is clearly readable. This may sound obvious, but any accompanist will tell you it needs to be said — loudly and frequently. No dark grey grunge from which the odd minim peeps shyly forth. 'Sorry, it wasn't a very good photocopier.' No skew-whiff copy whose jaunty angle means you didn't quite get the top left-hand bit in (which just happens to be where you find little details like tempo indication, time signature and key signature). Optimistic singers who say 'It's OK, isn't it? I got all the words in!' have victim written all over them.

- If you bring along a bunch of A4 sheets stapled on the top left-hand corner, expect the staple to be ripped ceremoniously from the music sheets. And know that you will have earned no brownie points from your accompanist.

CHARTS

A chart is not a score. Some wonderful accompanists can only read scores, and some equally wonderful accompanists can only read charts. Best you find out what your accompanist can work with before you front up with inappropriate material.

A vocal score has three lines of music. The top line gives the singer's melody (with the lyric words written under the music), while the two lines of music under it are the piano accompaniment. The start of a piano/vocal score might look like this:

Finding the family
(from "Hansel and Grethel")

By PAT WILSON

A chart contains a form of elegant musical shorthand, often used by jazz players and some rock and pop musicians. It's got the melody line, mostly in treble clef, which is for the singer. Above it, there is a line of alpha-numeric symbols such as F^7, G^{13}, $G^{\#}maj^7$ and so on.

These are the names of the chords which relate to each portion of the song. The musician reads the chart by playing chords appropriate to the melodic and rhythmic line laid out in the one stave of music. Sometimes the piano accompaniment is written in music notation as well.

A chart might look like this:

Finding the family
(from "Hansel and Grethel")

By PAT WILSON

As you can imagine, some classically trained pianists might have trouble working from a chart because they are used to playing from musical notation. Conversely, for the accompanist accustomed to working with charts, being presented with a piano/vocal score without chord markings can be equally distressing.

KEYS

Always be sure to sing in the key that best suits your voice. You wear shoes that are your size, and don't think twice about trying on lots of different shoes in a shop in order to get the smartest, the best fitting and the most comfortable. Your song should fit you like a shoe — a hand-made Italian one, preferably.

If you are working in an opera or a musical theatre show, it's unlikely that the musical director will rescore your solo for the 50 instruments in the pit band just because you're having a bit of trouble with the top note. It becomes your business to work hard on your range if you've been a bit lazy of late, or else prove to the management who hired you in the first place that they have miscast you.

However, when you have the chance to choose a song outside these rigorous circumstances, fiddle around until you find the key where you feel strongest and happiest. And then be prepared to negotiate: life is a series of negotiated compromises. Welcome to the big, wide world.

When you sing a piece in a key other than the one in which it is written, do try to perform it in what an accompanist would regard as an *easy* key. If you don't play a musical instrument or read music notation yourself, it's important for you to know what a musician might view as easy or difficult (*see* below).

Transposing

The first thing to remember is that if you've found yourself an accompanist who will instantaneously transpose, you have found a gem of great price. A treasure. Be nice to them, promise them anything (within reason). You're very lucky indeed. Many fine accompanists can only transpose a piece of music from one key to another by working out the new key, laboriously writing down what all the new notes will be and then playing from that re-written score.

Instantaneous transposition is the skill of looking at a piece of paper with the music written upon it in a certain key and promptly playing that very same music in another key, as required. The musician does instantaneous tranposition mentally. The intellectual process is akin to reading Swahili and giving a continuous colloquial translation into Spanish. It's an arcane, reasonably rare skill.

In my opinion, easier keys for pianists are:

MAJOR: C, G, F, D, B flat, E flat, A flat
MINOR: A, E, D, B, G, C

These keys have fewer sharps and flats in their key signature. This can only help the task of your transposing accompanist no end. They will thank you for this.

YOUR VERY OWN ACCOMPANIST

When you go for auditions, always ask whether you can bring your own accompanist along with you, or get your agent to ask the auditioning company for you. If it is permitted, and most of the large companies are fine about it, this allows you some control in an otherwise unpredictable territory.

BYO

No matter how terrific the company's audition accompanist may be, you're far better off with the security of your very own accompanist with whom you have rehearsed. This gives you the same comfort and courage that a violinist or guitarist derives from performing on the same instrument they have practised on at home.

A Chamber Group of Two

Don't think of your accompanist only when your agent tells you about a forthcoming audition and you hit the panic button. Doing regular sessions with your accompanist helps you both to build the rapport you need in order to blend well together. You will become a chamber group of two perceptive musicians who can second-guess each other's musical minds.

Working up your repertoire with your own regular accompanist is a good form of professional self-assessment. Having another person to work with is always a help. It's like having a chum that you always go to aerobics classes with — each of you helps keep the other keen. And who knows? Perhaps you can work up a nice two-hander cocktail act that will earn the odd dollar in between your other jobs.

Rehearsal Tapes

Another service which a skilled accompanist can offer is the preparation of specialised tapes to help you learn repertoire. If you don't read music very confidently yet, you may be having trouble learning the melody line of your songs and working out how that line fits against the accompaniment. Your accompanist can make rehearsal tapes for you, as described in Chapter 3, 'How to learn a song'.

Don't expect all this to happen for nothing: accompanists must be paid for their art, as must you when you work at your profession. But it's a modest investment for a large reward, especially if you have worked with your accompanist for some time. Together you will have established a musical subculture with its own language which you both know and use.

Your accompanist is a unique artistic ally: part interpreter, part parent, part lover. That's the best way I can explain this inexplicably close relationship. I wish you the joy of your very own accompanist.

CHAPTER 9

The Art of the Audition

*By some extraordinary fluke of an outraged glottis, she caught a high
note on a neap tide and held it. Like a draught horse stalled with a
heavy load on a hill, she held it. I shut my eyes and thought of knocking
off time at the steelworks and foggy nights on the harbour.*

Lennie Lower, *Here's Luck*,
Angus & Robertson, Sydney, 1930.

A uditions are a fact of life for every performer; part of the trade, whatever
your trade is. Actors, dancers, jazz singers, opera singers, rock singers,
recitalists and session singers will all find themselves having to audition in
order to obtain work. What's more, there are auditions for entry into drama
schools and conservatoriums, and the better you scrub up in an audition, the
better your chances.

Auditioning is an art. Although it's a performance-based art, there's more
to it than mere performance. Many a fine professional
performer will admit ruefully that they aren't good at
auditions, despite proven skills in their field. There are
no short-cuts to success; that's why we properly admire
the cream of the crop. I can, however, offer some hints,
suggestions, tips, clues and pointers: useful advice harvested from many a
weary auditionee who has staggered out of the audition room spluttering, 'I'll
never make that mistake again!'

> **An audition is a job
> interview**

If you view an audition as a sort of a job interview, you are more likely to
audition well. And as with any job application, preparation is 90 per cent of
the secret.

BEFORE THE AUDITION

Ask your agent to give you the show breakdown, so you can work out which
role/s you'd like to audition for, choose the most suitable song/s to sing and
how best to present yourself. A breakdown will list all the name roles in a
music-theatre piece and give a little character sketch about them, so that

agents don't send along petite 18-year-old blondes to audition for the part of Bloody Mary in *South Pacific*. Breakdowns are always useful, but for a new show, they are essential. No-one's seen it up and running before, so both your agent and you need all the help you can get in defining the auditioning company's requirements. How many songs? How long? Will I have to read as well? Or do a monologue of my own choice?

If your agent can give you little or no useful information about the audition requirements, contact the company yourself. It is important for your credibility in the industry that you present yourself for audition in a way that will not waste the audition panel's time. Are there roles in the show for a performer like you? Do you have to be able to rollerskate before you're even considered? Or tapdance? Or speak Hungarian?

A useful rule: unless specifically requested by the auditioning company, do not sing a song from the show you're auditioning for, even if it's your best party piece. The people casting the show may already have strongly formed ideas in their minds about just how they want to see this number done, and it's tough to audition your way past someone's prejudices.

Pick a piece that reflects the character of the part you're going for. You might be auditioning for *Oklahoma* and desperate to play the part of Ado Annie. It's no use singing, 'I Cain't Say No', but how about 'My Heart Belongs to Daddy' or 'Diamonds Are a Girl's Best Friend'?

Long songs, repetitive songs, boring songs — all these must be avoided. Some audition processes request performances of a given length of time. Never, ever exceed that time. Come in a bit *under* the specified time, if anything, and the panel will love you for that alone. If no time limit has been set, here's a practical rule of thumb: songs that are roughly as long as 'Stormy Weather' or 'When I Fall in Love' (once through, no repeats), are about the right length. Repetitive songs induce psychoses in audition panels.

It's a courtesy to give your accompanist as much help as possible (*see* Chapter 8, Working with Accompanists). Have a prepared copy of the score ready; mark it up in pencil with detailed indications sufficient to enable a pianist to support your performance. If your score is a sheaf of loose sheets of paper, join them accordion fashion.

THE NIGHT BEFORE THE DAY

On the night before your audition, there are a few things you ought keep in mind:

- Avoid air-conditioned premises. *Note:* Aircraft air-conditioning is notoriously rugged for the voice. If you must fly to an audition, try to get there 24 hours before you have to sound like a marketable proposition.
- Don't go out to hear a loud band, not even if you wear your semi-permeable ear-plugs. Tomorrow, in your audition, you will have to hear and pitch accurately.

- Stay out of smoky environments.
- Don't eat or drink dairy products for the 24 hours preceding your audition (they can induce mucus).
- Don't argue with anyone you love or live with. Save the drama for the audition panel and use it to get yourself a really wonderful job. Tonight, be sweetly reasonable to all God's creatures.
- Try not to take any medication for drying out mucous membranes for the 24 hours preceding your audition. Vocal folds have to be moist to be cheerful. If your nose is sniffy and drivelling, could a topical tramazoline hydrochloride nose spray (such as Tobispray or Spray-Tish) control the worst of the mucus until the audition is over? See if it can.
- Don't drink alcohol the night before, or for breakfast before the audition. Promise yourself a drink as soon as the audition's over.
- Don't smoke cannabis for *at least three days* before the audition.*

WHAT TO WEAR

When auditions are called, some companies specify the sort of clothing they would like you to wear. They may ask for things such as 'loose, casual clothing' (so you can roll around on the floor in a workshop session without compromising your freedom of movement or wrecking your best outfit), or 'dance clothing' (so that with close-fitting Lycra tights and leotard, choreographer and director can get a clearer picture of the line of your work as you move).

When clothing is unspecified, there are things that can help you and things to avoid when you prepare to audition — because it is with clothes that we can help people to see us in the way we want to be seen. Think about the part you want to go for. If you're female and you reckon you're perfect for the lead role of Heidi, the sweet, Swiss mountain girl, do something about your dreadlocks before you pop into the audition. Perhaps not a crocheted Rasta hat, either: try a blue-and-white gingham scarf over the wretched things. And prepare yourself to be asked if you're willing to cut them off and wear a blonde wig for the run of the show.

A balding male who wears a peaked cap is ill advised. You'll be asked to remove it by the audition panel; it won't want anything shadowing your face. Let's be blunt; it's got your promo photo already and it has a rough idea of your appearance (unless your photo is very old indeed — a serious lapse of professionalism). *And* they've asked you to audition — they must have liked what they've seen so far.

If you're going for a role in *The Sound of Music*, there's no real need to hire a pair of *lederhosen* in order to charm the audition panel. But it's no great hardship for a canny male performer to slick his hair down into the brilliantined style of the era before he goes in to audition. It's thoughtful,

---

*See Chapter 15, 'Friends and Enemies', for more details about the above points.

it's smart, it shows you're thinking about the show and its style.

Soft, flexible jazz shoes are good for both men and women to wear in an audition, even if there is little chance of your being asked to dance. They show your feet and emphasise your unique stance and gait. Thumping, great Nikes don't: they look like amorphous, white leather bandages on your feet. Yes, you're comfy. No, you don't show yourself off well. Stay comfy; stay unemployed.

It's smart to make sure that you have as little hair across your face as possible. The audition panel will generally want to know what your face looks like, unless you're auditioning for a hand commercial. If your hair is long enough, tie it back into a ponytail rather than having it flop across your face all the time. If it's not long enough, clips, gel, a scarf or a band should keep it off your face. If you've a fringe, make sure it's not so long or so heavy that it shades the upper part of your face. Cut it; slick it back; do something about it. Remember that most audition venues will have direct overhead lighting, which will immediately create shadow on your face if your fringe sticks out.

If you're desperate to advertise that you've a cascade of long hair, contrive to slip the hairband off it and (casually!) shake it out over your shoulders after you've done all your party pieces and just before you leave the audition room. Come on — you're an actor.

Don't wear fussy, ruffled collars that take up space between your shoulders and your neck. Keep the neck and shoulder area as uncluttered as possible.

Don't wear bracelets, earrings or ankle bracelets that jangle engagingly as you move. Busy professional people are trying to hear your voice; if they are forced to compete with a gratuitous percussion ostinato, they soon become annoyed and lose interest.

Whatever you end up wearing, make sure your mid-section isn't in any way limited by your clothing. Tight-waisted jeans, a smart, wide belt cinched up tight to show off your good waistline — these are going to obstruct your breathing and limit your freedom of movement.

WHAT TO TAKE

✓ Photo
✓ CV
✓ Your agent's or manager's business cards
✓ Accompanist's scores (at least one more piece than they asked for)
✓ Handkerchief or tissues
✓ Water

✓ *Photo, CV and Cards*

Take a spare promo photo (black and white, glossy, 8 by 10 inches [approx. 203 by 254 mm.], recent) and an up-to-date CV. Yes, yes, I *know* your agent will have already sent these through to the company when the audition was first arranged, but it never hurts to carry spares with you. I've known of occasions when photographs and/or CVs have become mislaid in the company's files, and if you turn up to the audition proffering copies of same, they'll be gratefully accepted.

This makes you look good and efficient, it ensures that your face and your details are up there with all the others, and you've got to take a briefcase along to the audition anyway to carry your music scores. Cards for your manager or agent are just another tiny detail that costs you nothing except the trouble to remember to keep a stack of them in your briefcase.

✓ *Scores*

Always take along one more song than the audition requires, on the good old something-up-your-sleeve principle. What if the audition panel goes dippy with delight at your audition piece and asks you to sing another, contrasting song? (It happens.) And what if, faced with this golden opportunity to prove your versatility, you stand in the middle of the audition hall and bleat, 'But you only asked us to do one song, dintcha?'

Resourceful auditionees will reach into their briefcase and pull out another, contrasting song. 'How would this one do?' they'll ask the panel. If the panel is happy to hear the piece suggested, you then take this marked-up copy over to the accompanist, with whom the wise auditionee will discuss its pitfalls and peculiarities before performing it.

Sometimes, when the panel sees you in the flesh, it may occur to it that you'd be perfect for a role other than the one you're auditioning for. An extra song with a different feel to it will keep you in the running.

Serious performers who are ambitious, keen and canny will always have more than one song up to performance standard. It's worth a stack of brownie points to present yourself professionally.

✓ *Handkerchief or Tissues*

When you leave home, you may feel in tip-top shape. By the time you get to the audition venue, your nose can sometimes resemble a leaky tap. Is it nerves, an allergy to traffic fumes, perhaps cigarette smoke breathed over you by a passing smoker? Whatever the cause, it's smart to bring a hankie or tissues.

Some folk always have a nice, big, cathartic cry after an audition — even if it went brilliantly! Performers tend to treat auditions like childbirth, forgetting the precise nature of the pains involved until it's time to face them all again. Working at a high-tensile emotional pitch for such a very short time means you'll be pretty worn out after an audition. Bring something to sniff into.

✓ *Water*

Don't tell yourself you'll grab a drink when you get there. Take a small plastic bottle of water with you. Not mineral water or a 'bubbly' (aerated) drink. It will make you burp forever. Your body runs on water; you can't sing without it. Your throat needs all the help it can get. Being self-reliant for water supplies is smart and saves you lots of worry and rushing around. Keep your energy for being stunning in performance.

GETTING THERE

Always go to an audition by taxi or by private car. OK, so you're poor. You can catch a bus or a train home. Or walk. *But* you've got to get the goods to market in the freshest condition possible, so always allow money for your taxi fare if you can't drive yourself to an audition or get a friend to drive you.

It's false economy to catch public transport and trudge wearily through the streets trying to find the address, getting more and more worn and frustrated. You're bleeding the energy and potential from your performance in just getting to the venue. It's too silly to contemplate, isn't it?

DOING IT

This is the moment! Fit, healthy, fully rehearsed and well-presented, you're about to prove to an audition panel how well-equipped you are to do the job they have on offer. But even though you've prepared thoroughly and feel confident about your skills, this is the time when almost every performer I know faces at least a twinge of nervousness. The more auditions you do, the better you'll get at judging your fear-management abilities. As part of audition preparation, you may find it useful to include some of the suggestions given in Chapter 7, 'Dealing with Fear'. Remember, there is a world of difference between being excited by adrenalin and disabled by terror.

When you arrive, you will probably be met by a stage manager who will take your name, check you off on the list of auditionees and perhaps give you a card to fill in. Know your phone number (even if you've just moved and only got the new number yesterday); have your MEAA/Equity card so you can cite your member number; have your agent's phone and fax details.

While waiting for your turn, try not to talk too much to other auditionees. There are three reasons for this. *One:* they may need to concentrate, and be far too polite to tell you to shut up. *Two:* you may need to concentrate and save your energy for the audition. *Three:* noise travels, and both performer and panel inside the audition room will hate the distraction of your nervous chatter.

When it's your turn, the stage manager will probably usher you through from the waiting room into the audition space. They may well introduce you to the panel members. If you're introduced, it's smart to take the time to shake hands on introduction and greet them by the name given.

Corny? Maybe. Smart? Yes, believe me.

Everyone on the audition panel is madly hoping that you'll be the one.

If you've ever been on an audition panel yourself, you'll know it's tough work. The audition panellists have committed much time and money to the search for the right person. If you're *IT*, their search is over. As each person walks through that door, the panellists are silently praying, please let this one be the right one. Walk in knowing they want you to get the job at least as much as you do.

If you haven't brought your trusty accompanist with you, the stage manager may next take you over to the piano where a total stranger who has heard everything from Pavarotti to a dying heifer will attempt to play the accompaniment to your song. This person will appreciate humanity, courtesy and professionalism. They will like being smiled at. Some performers will have treated them like a lower life-form. Dumb. This stranger can make you sound like a heap of trash or a stunning performer. Win their complicity and goodwill. Tell them all that they need to know; take your time explaining where you slow down, what repeats there are, if you hang on to the last note for a long time. The more you tell them, the better they're able to do their job. And if they do a bad job, you've got no chance of sounding good. And *you* miss out on work, not them.

AFTER THE AUDITION

When you've finished the audition, always thank the panel for its time. Whatever the outcome, the panellists have done you a favour already: they have given you the opportunity to stand in their shop window and perform. What's more, almost every audition panel I've seen is composed of a bunch of top-line people who are furiously busy and rarely get to sit in the same room with each other. Auditions are a privilege; do say thank you as you leave. And don't forget to thank the accompanist, too.

- They said, 'We'll let you know'.
- My agent knows nothing yet about any of the people put up for the show.

- My agent is sick to death of me ringing and asking.
- I'm getting neurotic. I can't focus on anything else, because all I frankly care about at the moment is getting *that* job on *that* show.
- Once I've heard — be it yes or no — I'll sort out the rest of my life.
- I'm sitting by my phone like a bad parody of a jilted lover.
- Can't I ring the company? the director? the producer? my cousin's sister who works as the production manager? Answer: no.

Wait.

CHAPTER 10

Rehearsals, Runs and Tours

*"Only the second-rate never make mistakes," he once teased. And again,
another version: "Only those capable of ugliness can be beautiful," a
phrase I had failed to understand, and thought nonsensical at the time.*

Peter Goldsworthy, *Maestro*,
Angus & Robertson, Sydney, 1989.

BEFORE THE FIRST REHEARSAL

Get out of bed three hours before you need to use your voice ... and that
goes for your speaking voice, too. Do you want a roomful of strangers,
some of whom are paying good money to hear your voice, to hear you sound
the way you do when you stagger straight out of bed and into your kitchen for
the first coffee of the day? So if rehearsals start at 10 in the morning, you're
out of bed by seven, even if you don't need all that time to launder, paint,
clothe and feed the body. Then drag it to the rehearsal room in time to arrive
at least 15 minutes before your call. The three-hour rule becomes barbaric when
you face a 9 am voice-over or a 6 am film-set call. There are times when this is
not a nice profession.

WHEN YOU'RE IN THE RUN OF A SHOW

Safety

Once you've begun rehearsals, get used to the concept of having been bought.
They've hired your skills, your sensitivity and your intelligence. And your
body. You're responsible for keeping the merchandise in good order — that
cheque you get every Thursday says so.

During the rehearsal period, and throughout the run of the show, try to do
nothing which consciously risks your health and safety. This is a large part of
what being a reliable performer is all about. Ice skating, rock-climbing, roller-
blading, sky-diving and horse-riding (especially steeplechase events and show-
jumping) are not on the recreational agenda now. Watch out for any activity
that might compromise your health (*see* Chapter 15, 'Friends and Enemies').

Sickness

If you sense the onset of a cold, a bout of the 'flu, the dreaded diarrhoea, any illness: off to the doctor with you. *Now.* Someone is paying for you; you're hired goods, and the likelihood of your being hired again, and thereby staying in your profession, hangs upon your being at least as good, as healthy and as reliable as you promised you'd be in your audition. Remember how well you presented yourself then? Keep the goods strong and fit for work, with the least downtime in rehearsals. It is agonising for other performers to have to work around you for a week or so because you can't give full voice while you're wrestling with a debilitating infection.

If your favourite remedies are holistic, long-term, non-interventionist healing ... you're too late! You can't afford to swallow garlic cloves and build up a nice healthy resistance to your ailment. *There's no time* : go to your GP and get something to reverse the course of your illness as quickly as possible.

Holistic remedies are often best, but the way they work is in organic harmony with your body, and at your system's own pace. This means that they will often fix you up more slowly than interventionist allopathic medicine. When you're in rehearsal or performance, you simply do not have the luxury of time. You have been hired as a working proposition. Tomorrow that's precisely what you've got to be.

Injury

Pulled muscles, stretched tendons, shin splints, skeleto-muscular problems are equally top-priority and must be attended to immediately. In the next break, phone your preferred osteopath, physiotherapist, orthopaedist or whomever you regularly trust with your aching bones or muscles. Make an appointment to see them as soon as you possibly can.

If your injury happened during rehearsal or performance, you must report the incident to your stage manager, director or manager. Even if it didn't involve any other person; even if it wasn't caused by you bumping into a brace or having a counterweight fall on you. The production must know about every injury. They have legal responsibilities as your employer, and also need to maintain a clear overview of their production at all times, including which of their troops is limping, and why.

The stoic performer who grimly carries on, never a whimper to anyone, and says to themselves 'After a nice, hot bath and a good sleep tonight, I'll be OK tomorrow', is a production problem. Any good director or choreographer can spot if you're working below your capability — they'll know something is up. Maybe they'll think you're having a lazy day. Perhaps they'll guess that you've hurt yourself, but you're too inexperienced or pig-headed to report it to management. It's unprofessional to do this to the production ... and to yourself.

By no means do a drama queen routine, scream, bellow for ice-packs and revenge, whilst dialling your insurance lawyer. This is too tacky to contemplate. But do advise your employer immediately if you've been hurt. 'She'll be right' does not apply in performance, ever.

Food

If your show starts at eight o'clock, make sure that you've finished your major meal for the day by 5.30 pm. Allow your digestive system a bit of time to make physiological sense of the fuel you've just given it. The body uses energy to digest food, and if you try to perform too soon after a meal, you can't access all your normal energy; some of it is sidelined into metabolism.

Another consideration is that a full stomach allows less effective space in your chest and abdomen for the work which the lungs will need to do when you sing. That filled-up feeling at the end of a meal is not any condition in which to do a show.

The best pre-performance food is nourishing, appetising and easily digested. Try to steer clear of greasy, hard-to digest food.

If you're doing both matinee and evening performances on the same day, you'll need to plan ahead how and what to eat between shows. It's unwise to go for two full performances without nourishment, but eating heavy stodge can slow you down remarkably. Top of the popularity list for between-show snacks are salads and vegetables, rice, steamed or grilled fish, chicken, a little ham, peanut butter, honey, Vegemite and fruit juices. In those productions which schedule back-to-back shows (with a one-hour turnaround), try to pick out the least likely foods to burden you from the company-catered between-show meal.

Do be careful when you choose food to eat before performance — and I don't just mean whether it's good for you or not. Much Lebanese food is remarkably nutritious; as take-aways go, it's one of the best a performer can get. But spare yourself the humiliation of green flecks all over your teeth after eating tabbouleh — it's not a good look. And passionfruit seeds can be just as subversive.

Health

Always buy yourself a bottle of vitamin C (ascorbic acid) powder or tablets at the start of rehearsals. Keep them in your rehearsal bag at all times. Vitamin C is not just for taking a fistful of if you think you might be coming down with a cold. It works as an antioxidant: it helps your body to manage toxin removal and it delays the degradation of single-tissue cells. It is every performer's most faithful ally.

When you buy the vitamin tablets, don't get the ones with no added sugar if you know you're unlikely to ever bother taking them. Even the most organically healthy tablets are useless if they stay in the bottle. It's better to suffer a bit of glucose and buy the munchy sort which you're much more likely to chew during the day. Or, if you're a hopeless wimp about tablets, get the big, fizzy tablets with the jolly flavours that you dissolve in a glass of water.

Take at least one a day for the duration of the rehearsal period, even on the weekends.

Health during the run of a show is a matter of preparation, not luck. Smart people keep healthy.

TOURING

When a show goes on tour, fresh challenges present themselves to the performer. It's a whole new ball game. There will be fiendish traps which will threaten to compromise your health as a singer. Shows that are as easy as pie when you're in a run in a theatre become a horror story when they hit the road.

- Travel itself can be traumatic. How many stand-up comedians make a living from ridiculing the trials of travel? You only laugh because it's as bad as they say. Waiting forever in airport transit lounges, going through customs, sea-sickness (or motion sickness of any kind), sitting up all night in a second-class train carriage, being a passenger in a car which is driven far too fast by an unskilled driver. Touring can be a bad trip.
- You may not be able to prepare your own meals in your hotel or motel.
- Meal times will be erratic and sometimes unpredictable.
- The drinking water in different cities may sometimes trouble your health.
- You have to adjust your performance to theatres or concert halls of different size, with acoustic responses ranging from glorious to horrible.
- You will have to do publicity calls. Cheerful media persons will interview you for their radio or television station or newspaper. They will ask you identical questions, while expecting you to look glamorous and sound coherent. You will have just done a three-hour plane trip, then a sound-check and feel like dying quietly in your hotel room.
- You may have to share accommodation with another cast or crew member. Will they snore? Or worse?
- Air-conditioning is everywhere — in planes, in hotels, in theatres. Its drying effects will need to be consistently fought.
- Most of your friends are somewhere else; you'll feel quite lonely at times.

The basic message about touring is this: if you need to be healthy, in peak physical fitness and perfect spiritual balance in order to do a performance, then double all that and you just might make it through to the end of a tour.

Travel Tips
- Never drink alcohol when you're on a plane. The pressurised cabin exaggerates the effect of the alcohol and gives you twice the hangover.
- Do your vocal warm-up in the performance space, even if it means getting in to the theatre far earlier than you really have to. You need to hear how you sound in there yourself, before you entertain paying customers. Check

times with your stage manager or tour director so you don't get in the way of the technicians.

- Try not to get into a routine after the show. It's always far too simple to set up a habit of going out with the cast and/or crew every night. When you don't feel up to it, they're all a bit put out, and you feel pressured to maintain the social contact as a matter of fitting in with the ensemble. In my experience, many of these folk will have eaten solidly before the show; you will not have. You'll feel hungry. They'll be looking for drinks and a good time; you'll need a wind-down after performance. It's good sometimes to go out with the gang, but it's smart to reserve your option to be just as likely to go off to your room or go out on your own.

- Always carry a sharp knife when you tour (no, not for homicide) also a vegetable peeler and your own knife, fork and spoon. Wherever you're able, get to the local shops and buy fresh fruit, vegetables that don't need to be cooked and a couple of pleasant staple items with which you can put together a light meal that you know you'll enjoy. Use your sharp knife to prepare the feast.

- With a little cunning, you can feed yourself quietly and very well in your own hotel room. It works out quite cheaply too, but cost's not the point. You have the luxury of preparing yourself, by being on your own, and eating favourite foods at the time you want to eat them. If your performance starts at 8 pm, you cannot eat at six o'clock. Yet 6 pm is the earliest that most decent restaurants open their doors. Before that, your meal choices are usually limited to take-away food: chiko rolls, hamburgers, fish and chips, a pizza perhaps. Dreadful fuel for singers.

- Suggestions for a shopping list: lettuce, tomato, capsicum, cucumber, mushrooms, celery, lemons (lemon juice is the perfect salad dressing), bread rolls or crispbread, ham, pressed cooked chicken slices, whatever fruit is in season and interests you.

- If you know you're going to be stuck in a car or train for hours and that you'll be unlikely to be able to buy reasonable food until you get to your destination, take your own travel snacks. Buy some dried fruit — sultanas, raisins, dried apricots, dried apples — whatever you fancy. Get a small packet of cashews, more almonds and even more peanuts (the ordinary salted peanuts are fine). Put them all together in a bag or container. Bring too much with you: your fellow passengers will loudly deny any interest in 'dreary, boring health food', then cadge another fistful from you.

CHAPTER 11

Vox Pop

As well as lacking a business brain, the band has musical problems.
Sharon can never be sure in advance whether Jason is going to sing or
not. He says he doesn't know himself half the time. His backing vocals
have a way of treading all over Sharon's lead vocals like a clumsy
partner in an old-fashioned tango. Sharon enjoys singing ballads; the
boys like playing up-tempo. Rollo keeps twiddling the dials on his
synthesiser when he's supposed to be playing piano, and often charges in
for a second chorus just as Sharon is about to sing.

David Foster, *Plumbum*,
Penguin, Melbourne, 1983.

Singing pop material uses exactly the same bits of your body as singing opera or 'Three Blind Mice'. Working as lead singer in a rock band is hard work; it's about as much effort as playing a principal role in a music-theatre production, and you have to keep just as well. Backing vocalists need to be able to dance and sing with equal stamina in conditions that are sometimes impossibly difficult. Many a conservatorium graduate who loudly despises the rock industry wouldn't have the strength to last the standard three-consecutive-gig test (Friday-Saturday-Sunday) out there in the real world.

A lot of people who say they are committed to carving out a professional career in the pop world are, in reality, optimistic hobbyists. On any given day of the week, in garages all over the nation, small groups of earnest, young performers huddle over guitar and keyboard, bass and drum kit. As they labour together to build that most elusive hybrid beast, a band, they will learn about the stresses of co-operation versus competition. They will find out about that nasty twitch towards the right which all lead guitarists' fingers develop when in contact with a volume knob. It's to be hoped that they will discover the almost magical quality which falls upon a band whose drummer and bassist enjoy and respect each other's work. Together, these twin pillars can build a strong structure of musicality within which the rest of the band may play and enjoy. There's a lot to learn. And lots to decide. Line-up? Covers or originals? Hire equipment and use profits to slowly buy your own, or wait until you've bought a basic minimum of your own gear before you perform? Manage yourselves? Get a manager? Work through an agency? Hire a sound engineer? Or get by with your cousin on the desk for $20 a gig? Look for recording contracts first? Do tribute stuff as a concept band, or else do covers until the money rolls in, then hit the market with your originals?

Get good advice from battle-hardened realists who are currently working in the contemporary music business, or who have a solid backlog of recent personal experience in the trade.

A BAND IS A JOB

Like all people in small businesses, band members have to plan a lot of dreary details. Once they're famous or rich, or preferably both, they'll have a manager, a host of roadies, a sound tech, a lights and rigging tech and the odd spotlight operator. Until then, it's the band members who have to see to getting bookings and hiring vans, people and a tonne of equipment. They have to sort out any technical problems, have to get everything to the gig in time to set up the hardware, run sufficient sound checks to satisfy everybody, make sure the light rig is up and going, reassure the management, make sure they'll get paid the agreed amount, do the gig brilliantly, bump all the equipment out quickly — especially if there's another band on straight afterwards — then return all hired gear promptly and in good order tomorrow morning at an indecently early hour.

People who work in rock bands are not lazy. Their commitment to their music and performance skills is such that they often become their own entrepreneurs, working intensely hard in order to keep doing the job they have chosen to do. When you audition for a band, don't be scared of looking too together, too organised, not laidback enough. A band is a job.

SINGING INTO A MICROPHONE

This is a skill which needs to be learned. It's best understood by doing it a lot, in much the same way as one learns swimming by jumping into the pool frequently. Some old rock 'n' rollers have never performed acoustically, while other singers have never even heard their voice through amplification and are terrified of singing into a mike.

If you have had little or no experience with amplified-voice systems, try singing into a microphone and listening critically to the resultant sounds through a good speaker system. Experiment with your sound; make funny noises; feel free to observe cause and effect. This direct information feed-back will help you to teach yourself quite rapidly how the process works.

From this you will discover that there is no need for you to bellow or bleat into that magical sound-catcher. Don't use it like a telephone, aiming all your sound into one little spot. This can strain your voice and strangle the quality of your sound. You will also fall into the nasty habit of forcing your tone by pushing air past your larynx. Apart from making yourself sound like an owl in mating season, all sound engineers will do anything to avoid you. Your plosives (the consonants that make little popping noises when you say them, like 'p', 'b', 't' and 'd') will pop and blurt onto the mike, and the resultant mix will resemble a broadcast from a battlefield.

Microphones do a specialised job: they have been designed so that you don't have to work so hard. If you have a good singing technique, you will hardly need to modify your usual voice when you sing into a mike. Skilled sound engineers know how to handle, decode, balance and mix the raw sound you serve up to them, as long as it is accurately and cleanly delivered to them.

Amp is short for amplifier. An amplifier is a machine for enlarging things. The microphone provides your only access to this system. Imagine the process of photo-enlarging a tiny Persian miniature painting. Every nuance, every delicate line with a two-hair brush will be clearly displayed once you've blown up that tiny picture into a huge photographic wall panel.

From this, two vital lessons:
1 Work accurately, work small, trust the amplification process and love your sound technician.
2 Tiny mistakes, when enlarged, become huge mistakes.

STAND ON YOUR OWN TWO FEET

Hangers-on

Try not to give in to the ever-present temptation to seize the microphone stand as you sing into the mike. This curious warning has little to do with posture, but a great deal to do with your freedom to use the power in your voice. There are a few suspicions that potter idly through an audience's mind when it sees a lead singer grabbing the mike stand and hanging on to it for dear life. 'I wonder if he's drunk?' is the first thing I think. Closely followed by, 'Nah, he's just terrified, I reckon'. Sometimes, if the singer refuses to let go of his chromium walking-frame all night, I conclude that the poor chap is older than he looks.

The Look

You may think you look sexy or impassioned or, on a good night, both. Hanging onto the mike stand is, however, a real sound-blocking activity. Perhaps you haven't given a thought to how you look — you're one of those boots 'n' all singers who refuse to think objectively about their performances. 'Ah, when I perform, I just let it all hang out.' How beaut for you. You don't have to see yourself, do you? However, your audience is paying to watch you as well as listen to you. It is elementary courtesy as well as good business to ensure that your customers are visually entertained (*see* Chapter 5, 'Dancing as a Singer').

Muscles and Nerves

Here's the main reason why you should stand on your own two feet: your true vocal folds are neurally connected to your biceps. Your false vocal folds are neurally connected to your triceps muscles. There you are, busy strangling the mike stand while you sing, and wondering why your voice isn't as strong and free as you know it could be. The nerve pathways linked to triceps and biceps get the story about your death-grip on the mike stand and pass that constricting tension down the line to your true and false vocal folds. Tension enters precisely where you need everything to feel as free and as open as possible. You think you're grabbing that mike in order to add passion and power to your voice, and all it really does is to restrict the range of your sound by forcing your vocal folds to constrict.

YOUR OWN MIKE

Half of Your Instrument

If you were a guitarist auditioning for a band, you would probably bring your own instrument along to the audition with you. Unless something extraordinary happened, you wouldn't think twice about bringing along the guitar you always practise on. It's the one that best displays your work; it is a basic component of your unique sound.

The same principle applies to vocalists. As a pop vocalist, your instrument is actually a two-part one — body plus microphone. So take along your favourite mike when you audition for a band. It has been your faithful companion in practice and performance; you know its sound profile and it enhances yours. It's smart to BYO, and good bands are more impressed with professionalism than the cultivated she'll-be-rightness of the chronically laidback. And never forget, it's the good bands that get work.

Styles and Mikes

Microphones come in a confusing array of qualities, sizes, sound profiles and prices. Some mikes add a sharp, metallic edge to your vocals; some of them warm and broaden your natural voice characteristics. Some of them make you sound as if you're standing on your head in a pickle barrel; some of them make you sound like a genius. Part of your art is to find the microphone which best complements your voice.

Recommended as the preferred type of microphone for pop work is the *dynamic* mike (as opposed to an electret condenser mike, a ribbon mike or an electret mike). Dynamic microphones have many virtues:

- They are least susceptible to 'handling' noise — the unwanted thumping or crackling sounds you sometimes get when you take a mike off its stand and move around with it.
- They tolerate a wider dynamic range; thus they are harder to overload or distort in the loud bits, while giving accurate pick-up for your softest sounds.
- They are physically more robust than other types of microphone and will withstand the onslaught of your standard electronic enemies, including moisture, lipstick, dust and ash, for longer before they start to sound like mud.
- They have a tight pick-up pattern. This means that they have to be worked close, but they won't easily pick up the rest of the cacophony on stage. As a consequence, your sound operator can exercise finer control of the vocals in the mix. By contrast, your average condenser microphone will hear the vocalist perfectly well, but will also pick up significant amounts of the other sound sources on stage. If you happen to be standing next to the piano or in front of the drum kit and your vocals need to be boosted in the mix, turning up your condenser vocal mike won't help at all — the competing sounds of the drums or the piano will also be turned up. This tight pattern in a dynamic microphone also means that the level of your vocal mike in the foldback can be higher before the sound begins to colour up and feed back.

It is practical to note that a quirk of dynamic microphones is their 'proximity effect': when worked very close, they have an improved bass response and add warmth to the vocal sound. If you work them at a distance, even only 15 centimetres (six inches) away, your voice will sound markedly thinner.

Shopping for a Mike

No two microphones will exhibit identical frequency response/tone quality. Not even in the same price range. If the technological side of it all is a bit much for you, enlist the aid of a friendly sound engineer who knows the trade. Get them to accompany you when you go shopping for a mike for yourself.

They'll be of invaluable assistance to you because some salespersons are much brighter at marketing than at musicianship and sound technologies.

Shops should allow you to test their mikes through an amplification rig, ideally in a special room or booth. There's just no other way of telling which mike you want. Reading the blurb on the outside of the box isn't much practical help. Ask them to let you try the mikes out — good shops will be happy to help you.

As you shop for your mike from supplier to supplier, remember that speakers can make a huge difference. Individual speakers, even when pumping out the same level, exhibit their own timbre. Because of this, the same mike used in the same way will sound very different when coming out of different speakers. Don't bother carting your own set of speakers from shop to shop; take a pair of good quality headphones with you, preferably the ones which have big closed muffs. These will give you the best chance to make accurate comparisons between microphones.

Your quest for the right mike may resemble Prince Charming's nationwide survey for the wearer of the fabled glass slipper. It might take you ages to find your perfect microphone, but the outcome is performance bliss. And happy-ever-after doesn't come to everyone, so it's worth persisting. Often, it's not even the most expensive microphone that's just right for you.

Considered against the costs faced by a keyboardist, a guitarist or a drummer, the cost of just one microphone is pretty modest. Yet it is half of your instrument; respect it as such. And thank your lucky stars when you have to de-rig after a gig: all you have to do is unplug your mike. Isn't it nice not being a drummer?

Care and Feeding

Microphones need to be looked after. There are some dynamic microphones which may still keep on working properly after being dropped or screamed into, but all mikes are designed to respond to vibrations — that's how they work. If the insides are made to move too far by meeting a concrete floor at speed, or perhaps by being blown into very hard, the internal diaphragm can tear or warp. This may mean that the microphone will not work, or else it might make you sound as if you have a clarinet reed stuck in your throat. Be nice to mikes.

Perspiration, saliva, hairspray, lipstick, sugary drinks and cigarette ash are amongst a microphone's worst enemies. They can build up in the mesh designed to protect the diaphragm and electronics, and will eventually deaden the sound. A snug-fitting, *acoustically transparent foam pop filter* is highly recommended. It should be removed regularly and washed in warm, soapy water, rinsed and completely dried before the next rehearsal or gig. These specialist foam microphone covers are more expensive than you might expect, but if you treat them well, they will last for years and prevent expensive damage to your microphone. I would be reluctant to buy a microphone if I couldn't find a foam pop filter to fit it.

REHEARSALS

Venue

The rehearsal venue is bound to affect the quality of your band's performances. If rehearsal space is cramped, the sound will be oppressively loud, no matter how you try to alleviate it. Try to get something that leaves the sound a bit of space to rattle around in, and that means not just floor space.

Older buildings made of stone or brick and with high ceilings and wooden floors are far better than modern structures with poured-concrete floors, low ceilings and, at best, brick veneer wall structure. You'll be glad of something which insulates your sound from the neighbourhood (and most neighbours feel that way too). The old pressed-metal shed with a poured-concrete floor, no ceiling, no insulation and a low roof is deadly. This way madness lies.

Rig

Always rehearse with as much gear as you can. Don't be lazy. Part of the art of contemporary music involves the interface between hardware, technologies and the tradition of creative human music-making. If you will be using a mike on a stand in performance, set it up and put it through an amp in the rehearsal room.

Ignore any band members who will themselves play with electrically boosted sound whilst denying you the courtesy. Would a guitarist playing a solid-body electric guitar not bother to plug into an amp because it's just a practice? And will the synth player spend the practice time sitting and thumping his keyboard, swaying and grinning, while his total sound output goes though his earphones alone? Hardly. Not for a band practice. When you rehearse, you all need to hear each other, learn each other's sound idiosyncrasies and spark off each other creatively. Without amplification, you won't be heard on parity with the other instrumentalists.

> **A band is a job**

Your voice is only half your instrument, and all the band needs to hear your total instrument, so set up your mike (preferably owned and loved by you), your mike stand (standard or boom), run it through your amp equipment and *rig yourself a dedicated monitor speaker* so you can hear precisely what you're up to. Yes, even in a rehearsal.

With a foldback speaker (or monitor, wedge or whatever you are used to calling this piece of life-saving equipment), you will prevent the possibility of screaming to hear yourself over the rest of the band's sound. It's impossible to control and assess wisely the fine judgements required of a singer when there's a high level of background sound and you can't hear yourself. After a while, you simply get paranoid and squawk at the top of your tortured lungs in a desperate if vain attempt to hear what you're up to. This is a process which will guarantee you awful damage to your vocal equipment. Whisper the word 'nodules' and watch any professional singer turn pale and run.

Safe Singing

Always wear semi-permeable ear-plugs when rehearsing with your band. Sometimes, the rehearsal conditions are far more dangerous for your hearing than the gigs themselves.

When you perform in a large space, with an acoustically tiled roof and a good speaker stack well tuned and laid out, the sound is entirely appropriate and sits well within the enclosure. If you rehearse for that gig in your uncle's galvanised-iron garage, you run the clear risk of hearing loss. And that's death to any singer. Always wear semi-permeable ear-plugs when rehearsing with your band. I know I said it before: most rock musicians need to be told twice; they can tend to be a little hard of hearing. Funny, that.

BEFORE THE GIG

Bump-in

Be prepared to help your band bump in; to load a hired van, or a few long-suffering station wagons, with speakers, desks, kilometres of cable, light trees, mike stands, DI boxes, tool kit and the musical instruments to cart them to the venue. Be prepared to find someone who will unlock the venue for you if it's not opened as they promised you it would be when you spoke to them last week. Be prepared to carry all your hardware into the venue (many venues have stairs; few have goods lifts). Then, set it all up, plug it in and check that it works and looks and sounds right, and to everyone's satisfaction. Full rig and full sound-check means that you can all go home feeling confident about the forthcoming night's performance.

Although you, as a vocalist, have the privilege of carrying your instrument internally, the band will expect you to assist with the hard work involved. You'll take a share of the profits, so it's only fair for you to muck in with everyone else.

Dress Code

Here's what the well-dressed band member wears for a bump-in: rubber-soled shoes, dark, grungy, close-fitting clothes (the sort of stuff you can get dirty in) and mechanist's gloves, especially if you are a guitarist.

No Sound-check, No Gig

Never, ever perform with any sound-reinforcement or microphone of any kind unless you get a sound-check beforehand in the venue with the equipment which will be used in performance. Be utterly rigid on this. It's your reputation on the line and no-one else's. Because of the work you do as a vocalist, everyone looks at you when the sound quality is vile. Few people in the crowd will say, 'My, what a hopeless sound engineer!' They're more likely to ask, 'What's wrong with that singer?'

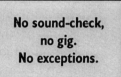

No sound-check,
no gig.
No exceptions.

Yes, this is unfair. But that's how it goes. No sound-check, no gig. No exceptions.

Love Your Sound Engineer

Make sure that you have a good rapport with your sound engineer. They can make you sound like a million dollars; they can also make you sound like trash. It is entirely in your own best interests to be extremely nice to your sound engineer. Get to know them as a person and allow them to get to know you. This is not half-baked hippie psychology: this is street-wise band politics.

If the sound engineer knows the sort of person you are, and knows that you respect them as a performer in their own area of musical skill, then they can mix your voice intelligently. They will know how to place your vocal work within the blend of the band so that the resultant profile is a recognisably unique and attractive signature sound.

Put a sound engineer's nose out of joint and you can find yourself suddenly unable to hear anything through your foldback speaker. Who knows what they're pumping out to the audience through the sound bins. If you've upset your sound engineer, don't expect them to be working hard at making you sound your best. A good sound mix is a sort of cosmetic treatment for the amplified voice. It can make ordinary singers sound magnificent. Never forget that the reverse can also apply. Love your sound engineer.

THE GIG

When you arrive to do a gig at a pub or other band venue, you will very rarely find jolly little backstage dressing-rooms where you can get dressed, do make-up, warm up your voice with a few gentle arpeggios and keep yourself calm and unflustered until the performance. The venues that have these refinements are rare and much loved by performers. The dreadful reality is you turn up ready to go, you do your act on stage, you unplug your gear and pack it back in your van, find someone who will pay you (good luck), and then high-tail it out of there. That's it.

The Toilet as Refuge

Bands which have a highly theatrical approach (pyrotechnics, bizarre costumes, heaps of stage props and so on) become very ingenious in the use of pub toilets. The loo is your only hope if you feel shy about driving to your gig dressed as a two-metre-tall crayfish. There are, I must admit, a few public toilets I'd think twice about entering dressed in civvies and with a big rubber crustacean costume over my arm, but that's showbiz.

Again, the loo is your only hope for a vocal warm-up. You won't be able to warm up in the venue when the previous act is on, or the PA is grinding out recorded music in between live acts. The smoke, the extraneous sound, the fact that persons near you will think you are feeble-minded — all this must drive you to the toilet. Into a cubicle, shut the door and stand there doing your vocal warm-up. Of course, it's not an ideal situation, but it's far better than performing unprepared. Sometimes, the distance between your home and the venue means that the good workout you may have given your voice in the privacy of your own space will feel as if it happened a long, long time ago.

Water

Make sure you take your big bottle of spring water with you; it's best to be self-reliant in the matter of water supply. When you ask for water at a pub, many can give you only soda water or mineral water (burp fodder), or a glass of water out of the tap. In some places, the tap water is unspeakable: in Australia, Adelaide and Brisbane are good examples. Even the knowledge that you really need to hydrate your system cannot overcome the sheer awfulness of the tap water. BYO is the smart rule.

Between Sets

If your band is doing more than one set, what do you do between sets? This is not as silly a question as it may at first seem. Band work demands a huge energy output allied with a high order of concentration. All of this has to be delivered in an informal style which looks as if you aren't trying hard to do anything.

If the venue is air-conditioned, try to get outside for at least a bit of your break in between sets. If the venue is not air-conditioned, but smoking is allowed, you're also smart to head outdoors in your break, even if you're a smoker. The high concentrations of passive smoke will harm your vocal flexibility pretty quickly, and your only hope to get through the whole three sets without your voice croaking is to grab a breath of fresh air.

If your costume and make-up render you a figure of fun, it's impossible for you to wander too far outside, but do try to get out of the four walls, away from the sound intensities, and regroup your strength for the remainder of the gig. If your band has a strong following, and audience members are expecting to see you mingling with them between sets, try to do this at the end of your set for just a short while; then slip away in the best traditions of espionage. If you're cunning, they'll never notice.

CHAPTER 12

Sound Studio Notes

Every playing of a record is a liberation of a shut-in meaning — a movement, across the groove's boundary, from silence into sound, from code into clarity. A record carries a secret message, but no one can plan the nature of that secret, and no one can silence the secret once it has been sung.

Wayne Koestenbaum, *The Queen's Throat: Opera, Homosexuality and the Mystery of Desire,*
Penguin, London, 1993.

Here, in note form, are a few suggestions to help make a singer's visit to the recording studio as trauma-free as possible.

WHAT TO WEAR

Clothes
Wear plenty of layers. Air-conditioning can make the studio temperature nothing like the temperature outside. You'll heat up during takes; you'll cool down while you wait for engineers and producers to complete technical tasks.

Jewellery
Avoid wearing dangly earrings, jangly bracelets or beads or noisy jewellery of any kind. Even silent (non-dangly) earrings aren't a good idea: with the exception of tiny studs and sleepers, you'll only have to take them off if you're using headphones.

Smells
Don't wear perfume, scent or aftershave. Even if your perfume doesn't irritate you, there are other people to consider. Remember that you'll be working in a recycled-air environment.

HOW TO SING IN A STUDIO

Sing the way you usually do. If you're not accustomed to working in a studio, it's likely that the engineer will run a compressor across your recorded voice to ensure that the equipment will be able to handle your dynamic range. Singers who are used to studio work can often modify their sound so that its profile most suits the recording task. This skill takes many hours of experience to learn, so sing like you usually sing and let the engineer fix the technical end of things.

Hint for Backing Singers

Don't oversing; there's never any need to push your voice. Your sound is being set against the featured soloist's and therefore your vocal intensity will need to be less. Listen to your engineer's instructions, so they don't have to compress the vivacity out of your sound in order to balance the final mix.

CAN DO

It's rare for a singer to work in a sound studio without having to use earphones ('cans') so you might as well make friends with them.

Getting Used to Headphones

If you've never sung while wearing headphones, get used to them before you go into the studio by practising singing while wearing them. The mere fact of singing with your ears covered can be disconcerting at first. Headphones alter the way you monitor your own sound and they take a bit of getting used to. A simple simulation: use Mickey Mouse ears. Cupping your hands behind your ears is an easy way to experience your vocal sound arriving at your ears at a different angle.

Happy with the Mix

In the studio, make sure your headphones are delivering a good mix. Can you hear the music to which you have to sing? Not too loud, not too soft, but just right? Has the sound got reverb or other effects on it? And do you like it like that? Can you hear your own voice clearly enough?

Never attempt a take until you are happy with your headphone mix. Don't be afraid to pester the engineer until you are comfortable with both volume and bass/treble balance of the sound that reaches your ears. You've got to be able to work with it. There may even be a time when you have to ask the engineer to leave the control room and listen to what you're getting through your headphones, in order to sort out faulty sound delivery.

Hint: When some singers are doing harmony work, they prefer to work with one headphone off the ear. If you do this, remember to slide the earpiece *behind,* not in front of your ear, so you don't get feedback from your microphone.

STUDIO MIKE TECHNIQUE

Learning Mike Technique

The best way to learn is by using a microphone in live performance. These circumstances allow you to assess, in collaboration with your sound engineer, what best suits your voice and your tastes. The instant cause-and-effect result of tweaking a sound rig in live performance can be a speedy educational tool, if initially alarming to singers unaccustomed to working with a microphone.

In the studio, one learns about microphones but less swiftly. It is hard to gauge the effects of different control settings when you don't get to visit the control booth very often. In addition, your headphones are designed to give you just enough quality of sound to sing with, whilst allowing you to still hear your own voice. Working live with a microphone is the quickest and surest way to build effective mike technique.

Height

It is simply bad vocal practice to sing bending down, with your chin scrunched onto your chest. It's equally useless to sing with your head tilted up to a too-high mike. Allow the engineer to place the microphone at *exactly* the right height for you.

Position

Some people like to stand up when they sing in a studio. Some people prefer to sit and sing. An engineer friend of mine says he knows a number of singers who prefer to sing in the recording studio while lying on their backs. He's happy to rig their microphones accordingly. Once you're used to working in a recording studio, and know how you like to work your sessions, it is courteous to advise your engineer ahead of time of your technical requirements.

Distance

You don't have to be on top of a mike. Where do you stand? Ask the engineer; they'll tell you. The engineer will know the specific mike requirements of your voice.

Pop

There should be a pop cover (a piece of circular gauze) between you and the microphone if the singer's work threatens to be fairly wordy and filled with plosives ('p', 'b', 't', 'd' sounds).

DIRECTION AND ADVICE

In a recording studio, producers and engineers will offer you guidance. Their comments may seem understated little observations, so mild and casual that you'd hardly take notice of them.

These people will talk to you in a totally different way from the way directors in theatre or opera do. There's rarely any hand-waving, perspiring or yelling from studio staff. Producers and engineers tend to be gracious people of few words, but their succinct style carries much authority, and it's handy to be able to decode their laidback language.

Here are a few sample comments. Anyone who has worked in recording studios will recognise at least some of these:

- 'That was lovely, but I reckon there's a better one in there.'
  Translation: Not good enough. Do it again.
- 'Wasn't that great? Let's do it again!'
  Translation: Not good enough. Do it again.
- 'Just one more for me, please.'
  Translation: Nearly good enough. Do it again.
- 'That was a terrific middle eight.'
  Translation: The rest of it was not good enough. Do it again.

The pattern is almost universally *A positive statement* followed by *directorial information*. It's smart to take the information on board. Producers and engineers can hear more than you can.

TAKES

Don't burn out on too many takes. If the track you're doing just doesn't seem to be working, move on. The engineer or producer is likely to suggest this to you at a time when experience predicts that you're less likely to come up with the goods by persisting than by going on to another track and returning to this one later.

You may feel that you should stick doggedly to the job in hand. 'I hate quitting.' 'I won't let this beat me.' You don't want to be seen as a failure, but you'll probably waste valuable studio time if you insist on being compulsively conscientious.

Take the advice of the experts. Go on with something else. There are times in a studio when more work on the same track merely moves you further away from your goal. Skilled engineers and producers know this phenomenon well. It happens to everyone.

You may have to revisit some stubborn tracks quite a few times. Patience! Never let your exasperation get the better of you, and try not to walk away from a project until you've got a performance that pleases you.

THE WORKING ENVIRONMENT

Comfort

This is the key word for studio work — get comfortable. Never be afraid to ask for anything that will help you feel more comfortable. As much as is possible, both engineer(s) and studio assistant(s) will attempt to adjust the working environment so that it best suits your needs.

Paranoia

Studios can have an alienating air about them; you're in one room, often all by yourself. The engineer(s) and producer(s) are in another room filled with techno-trickery. They stare placidly at you through thick glass; you feel like a goldfish. They can hear every breath you take; you can't hear them unless you ask them to switch on the intercom, when a booming voice fills your headphones. You look at them chatting, gesticulating, laughing in the control booth. Are they laughing at you? Are they saying, 'Pathetic. Thinks s/he can sing. Can't wait till this one is over'? You can get quite paranoid.

Be prepared for the fishtank effect in a studio by making sure you strike up a good communicating relationship with the technical staff before you get shut away to work. By the time you're speaking to them *via* intercom, they'll have some idea of your personality, your concerns and hopes for the session. If they are good at their profession, they'll want to put you at your ease and keep you there, because they know you're only likely to provide top-quality sound under those conditions.

Always ask

Never be afraid to ask questions. There are, however, two rules to be observed:

1 Ask nicely.
2 Try not to ask questions when the studio staff look very busy.

WHEN YOU HIRE A STUDIO

Cost

Always ask how much the studio charges before you turn up ready to work ... unless you're very rich. Check the per-hour and the per-day rates. Ask what the hire fee includes: does it cover everything, or do you have to pay extra for the engineer at an hourly rate? How about consumables, such as tapes? Only when you know all the financial facts, and have come to a clear, negotiated agreement with the hirer, is it safe to start your recording session.

Time

If there's a time of the day or night at which you're happiest to sing, hire the studio for that time. Night owls are particularly grateful that the recording industry isn't a nine-to-five trade.

Atmosphere

When you want to put together a demo tape that showcases your voice, it pays to work in a space you like with people you trust. You'll cut down on studio time and end up with a better product.

Knock on doors, visit different studios and talk to the people working there before you decide where to go. You'll soon work out whether you'd feel comfortable and relaxed working with these people in these environments. Always ask yourself if you're working with the kind of people who are likely to like what you do and encourage you towards your best performance.

Even when 'people who know' tell you that you should do your sessions in this faaabulous studio they know about, reserve your judgement until you've been there and talked to the staff. Trust your feelings.

Which Mike?

If you don't have your own pet mike (*see* Chapter 11, 'Vox Pop') to take along to your sessions, ask the studio you've chosen to work with to set up three or four of their best vocal microphones before your first session. Begin by using all of them for a few minutes each, recording the sound. Listen carefully to the tape, then listen carefully to the engineer's advice, and then you'll be able to choose the microphone which gives you the best sound for your purpose.

Three tips:

1 If you want to do comparative testing, always advise the studio at least a week before your first session, so that the engineer can allow time for the set-up.
2 It is wise to make a written note of the microphone (make and model) that you end up choosing to use. If it's so good, you should always ask for it whenever you record in future and perhaps consider buying one for yourself.
3 Don't expect any studio to go to this much trouble for a 'quickie' half-hour session.

CHAPTER 13

Voice Exercises

The warm-up was as effective as any warm-up before any game. We were ready to take on the songs we sang as if those songs were opponents and we were a team. Breathe in, hold, one two three four ... breathe out, slowly, seven six five four three ...

Timothy Doyle, 'A Choir Story' in *Red Hot Notes*,
Carmel Bird (ed.), UQP, Brisbane, 1996.

The word 'exercise' carries with it echoes of the dull thud of duty. The idea that a serious vocal performer must daily trudge the solitary path of voice exercises is frequently seen as a major turn-off by prospective vocal professionals. Your development of stamina, flexibility, tone and repertoire is, however, dependent on more than a lesson a week with your singing teacher or vocal coach, no matter how wonderful they might be. Merely singing songs will not teach you the subtleties of the craft.

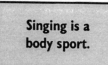

Singing is a body sport.

Singing is a body sport. The physical discipline involved in the patient build of a dancer's skill is a good parallel to the body discipline of singing. Part of the work of being a singing performer includes such tasks as building neuro-muscular skills and muscle mass, enhancing physical flexibility and promoting agility. The need for short, regular, effective exercise sessions becomes more obvious when you tackle singing as a sort of sport.

If you are serious about working as a singing performer, you need to be able to keep the physical mechanism in shape, in just the same way as professional dancers get rusty if they don't do regular classes every week.

A word of caution. Some people boast of doing long, gruelling exercise sessions. If you are not a very experienced singer and you spend more than, say, 15 minutes a day on your voice exercises, it is possible that you are doing too much. Caruso used to say 'Until they become thoroughly proficient in managing the voice, pupils should never devote more than fifteen minutes a day to practice.'

If you don't quite have the hang of a particular voice exercise, and you practise it incorrectly for five minutes daily, there's no great damage done. If, however, you hack away at the wretched thing for a full half-hour a day, you will have built up a considerable backlog of incorrect technique. This will take some effort to dislodge when next you have a session with your singing teacher. Unsupervised practice can be less than beneficial.

It is not within the scope of this book to provide voice exercises which, if you do them a sufficient number of times a day, are guaranteed to transform you from a vocal wimp to a top-rate singer. Your singing teacher or vocal coach can devise the right sort of exercise program for you. If it's correctly tailored to your personal strengths and weaknesses, 10 minutes of that will be worth more to you than an hour's huffing and puffing through a set of vocal press-ups that don't address your own needs and that you run the risk of performing incorrectly.

THE FOUR PROBLEMS WITH EXERCISES

1. I Can't Get any Privacy

Privacy is hard to get these days. The last bastion of visual privacy is the loo; and the last bastion of aural privacy is the private motor car.

But sitting in a car isn't the best way to get regular voice practice.

Everyone starts off feeling somewhat awkward about other people listening to them while they make what sounds like an effects sound-track for a film about abattoirs. If you live on your own, you have no worries, unless you live in a flat with thin walls. Singers pray for profoundly deaf neighbours — don't we all?

If you live with others, you can always wait for everyone else to go out and then do your vocal practice. This may take some time, especially if you live with indigent or agoraphobic people. Ever shared house with an unemployed, depressed TV addict?

Consider the idea of singing while they're in the house. Let 'em suffer! Perhaps there are things that they do to your soundscape? Do they ask your approval before they turn on the radio or play a CD or switch a TV channel? Tell yourself that your voice is just another sound source around the homestead, and now and again you have been called upon to suffer: ☐ King Crimson ☐ James Last ☐ Mahler ☐ John Denver ☐ Barbra Streisand (you may tick more than one) without being consulted by your flatmates. Vengeance!

2. I Haven't Got a Piano

How to remember all those voice exercises your singing teacher gave you? The fiddly arpeggios and the weird intervals? How to know where to start? And how about the sense of triumph when you find out that you've just hit a top A flat? Without a keyboard or similar instrument, how do you know when you reach it?

You probably need a tape of piano accompaniment for all your vocal exercises. You will want it to go at a pace that suits you and have no vocal sound on the tracks. You will need to listen intently to your own voice whilst exercising, and the sound of another voice (even your own) is likely to throw your concentration off centre. When you sing along with another human voice, you're tempted to simply duplicate what that recorded voice does, rather than work objectively on your own voice. Because of this, it's no use digging out a tape of one of your old lessons and singing along with that.

A sensible solution to your problem could be taking one or more of your old lesson tapes along to a good accompanist and asking them if they could help you to put together an exercise tape — as long as you explain to them exactly what you want (*See* Chapter 8, 'Working with Accompanists').

3. I Sound Awful when I Do My Exercises

Relax and rejoice! We all do, now and again. If performing a song is like a studio glamour photograph, then exercises are like X-rays. No-one looks cute in an X-ray, but they show you where your weak spots are. Good voice exercises are diagnostics which highlight the flaws in your vocal range. Now, there may be days when you don't feel up to hearing all that undiluted honesty, but remember that the greatest voices can sometimes make pretty bad sounds. The smart thing that those great singers do is to make all their unsavoury noises in private exercise sessions, so that they're sure they'll never emerge during performance.

4. I Get Bored with Exercises

Forget a professional career in performance.

HEARING YOURSELF

While preparing your body and voice for the intense demands of singing, you will often wish that you could listen to yourself more clearly. Sooner or later, all serious performers pray the modified Robbie Burns prayer: '... to hear ourselves as others hear us'.

Unfortunately, recording cannot deliver this blessing. A tape of my voice can only tell me how I sound to a machine. However sophisticated that machine may be, it is limited in its ability to collect my sound, encode it and then faithfully reproduce whatever it was able to capture. People hear differently. Unless you're preparing for a stint in a recording studio, a tape can give you only a rough indication of how you're going.

How, then, can you hear what you're doing as objectively as possible? The problem lies in your head. This place where so much tone generation and resonance occur is also the same bony cavity in which our hearing equipment is housed. Forget objectivity while all that resonance rattles through your skull. The vibrations of your voice affect your hearing while you're trying to listen to yourself.

There are a few easy tricks which singers resort to in an attempt to analyse their own sound.

Koala Ears

While you sing, hold your hands in front of your ears, palms facing backwards and thumbs on the outer edges; don't cup your hands. Look in a mirror and you will understand the name of this lurk. You will hear your voice 'at a remove' — diverted by your hands, the sound will arrive at your ears by a more circuitous route than usual.

Standing in the Corner

If you stand facing the corner of a room and sing into it, the sound bounces back at you. Stand right *in* the corner, as if you were a child being punished; your face should be very close to the walls. This works best when the corner has no curtains, windows, bookshelves or suchlike, just the meeting at 90 degrees of two unadorned hard surfaces.

Combine this one with the koala ears (above) and you should have a lot of extra useful information about how your voice sounds.

> **Your body shapes your sound.**

Chairs

Put a chair on your head and sing. Find a *light* chair with an uncushioned seat, preferably one of those cheap, plastic stacking chairs with a continuously moulded back and seat. Turn it upside down, so that its legs are pointing at the ceiling. Place it on your head, as if it were a hat. The back of the chair should extend down your back. Steady this eccentric piece of head-gear by holding onto each side of the seat with your hands. Now sing.

Your voice is intercepted on its way to the ceiling and bounced back to you by the chair seat. The sonic information you derive from this process is different from the other two techniques mentioned above, because it reflects back sound from above you rather than modifying the way your ears hear your slipstream sound. It does, however, provide equally useful information, and is a particularly effective trick for picking any forced or strained production in your tone.

Some people may feel stupid popping an upside-down chair on their head and then singing. I find that these are, almost without exception, singers who have never worked in opera. If you have ever been called upon to wear an opera costume, even as a supernumerary, nothing will surprise you again as long as you live.

TOO TIRED

There will be times when everything will get too much for you, but you must still keep your voice in shape. A frantic schedule, poverty and performance stresses are a combination sufficient to undermine your physical and emotional strength. But you must still get that instrument of yours out of its case frequently and regularly; you can't afford to let it get rusty. There are a couple of useful tips to help you overcome your reluctance to exercise:

Useful Tip 1

Lie down on your back on the floor and do your usual range of vocal exercises and warm-ups. Once you lie down, draw your knees towards your chest and then return your legs flat to the floor, or else lie with bent knees. This ensures that your lower spine gets unkinked when you lie down. Do the same favour for your head and neck: once you're lying down, raise your head and roll it back gently onto the floor, allowing any kinks in your neck to undo themselves.

Most of the back muscles of your thorax are supported by the floor when you lie down. Consequently, you automatically halve the amount of hard work your chest muscles have to do as you sing. You will find that things you never quite had enough breath to complete are easier to sing. You can do those great long phrases with freer breath — it's all a lot less strain and pain.

Unfortunately, there are few gigs which will require you to lie on your back — in the legitimate singing industry, anyway — and so this is an inappropriate regular practice technique. But it's a great help when you feel reduced in strength and health, and, what's more, it's a pleasant sensation feeling the resonance of your voice buzzing beneath you, especially on wooden floorboards.

Useful Tip 2

Lie on your stomach and do a selection of your usual resonance and frontal placement exercises. This one works best on a clean, hard floor — your kitchen floor, perhaps. It's not good to bury your nose in the fluff and dust-mites of your carpet. Lie on your front, legs straight, resting your forehead on your folded hands, so that your nose is not on the floor but nearly so (now you know why the floor needs to be clean).

The kind of resonance you receive back from the floor as you sing will overwhelm you at first. If you haven't tried this trick before, you will be surprised at the strength and texture of your voice. This is the sound which, under normal (that is, vertical) circumstances, falls straight out of your face to your audience. Now and again, especially if you're feeling tired and a bit weak and ineffectual, remind yourself of the innate power of your voice by listening to yourself in this way.

PRE-PERFORMANCE WARM-UPS

Mark Baxter has a radical aphorism I like a lot. In *The Rock-n-Roll Singer's Survival Manual,* he says, 'The longer the performance, the shorter the warm-up' (p. 220). This sounds like a sort of cop-out if you're doing a huge show, but the fact about huge shows is that they're technically demanding. You'll have had to do tech run after tech run to get the lighting plots right, to fix any bugs in the sound, to check costume changes, to make sure you're happy about singing in the space. (You will need to get the acoustic fingerprint of the enclosure so you can work it happily and well.) That lot will have warmed you up good and proper, if not worn you out.

Two hours before you go on stage is not the time to give your vocal folds a knock-down-drag-out exercise bout. Light and seamlessly smooth movement between your high, middle and low sounds, followed by a couple of your favourite exercises to regulate your breathing will be about all you need to do.

It's too late now to attempt that monster high note you mostly got in rehearsals but sometimes botch. Forget it. Or, at most, do all the physical work of singing that note perfectly, *but without any sound at all,* whilst leaving your throat wide open and relaxed. Just two or three of those soundless top notes should be sufficient.

Concentrate now on your focus: rolling your energy and presence into a tiny, highly compressed ball. It's smart to try and set up whatever circumstances you find best to prepare your heart, head and body for the tasks ahead. Many performers gain better focus and energy from sitting quietly and calmly gathering their wits before the show.

For cool-down exercises please *see* Appendix 2 (page 112).

CHAPTER 14

A Body to Sing With

Singers are the Olympic athletes of the voice world.
Professor Robert T Sataloff, MD, DMA,
Third Australian Voice Symposium, 1995.

S inging is a curious profession. You dwell constantly with your tools of trade. You sleep with your musical instrument, you take it to the beach. Bus, train, car or bike — it is always with you. You take it with you to parties and never go on holidays without it.

Your *whole body* is your instrument, not just your neck. Don't get fixated on those little pictures of cricoid cartilage, false folds and naso-pharyngeal what-have-yous. These structures help originate your sound, but your musical instrument is your whole body.

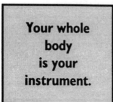

Your whole body is your instrument.

You are issued with your voice at birth. Some folk get really fine ones, while others get pretty ordinary ones. You'll find that the greatest singing performers in any field are not always those blessed with structurally fantastic voices. Likewise, many folk who were born with vocal instruments of great natural beauty and strength never, ever sing. They don't want to — that's how it goes.

Knowing that the instrument that produces your voice is your entire body, it makes sense to take good care of all aspects of the body you sing with.

TEETH

For a singer, teeth are indispensable. They're very much in evidence whenever you work. Because of this, they have to look good. Their shape helps determine the resonance and timbre of your vocal sound. And because toxins cause all manner of health problems, rotten teeth can slow your career down, too.

Amalgam (Mercury) Fillings

These are the old-style silvery metallic dental fillings which, after a while, turn black. Television and film cameras work so closely to your face that you cannot afford to have any amalgam fillings in your teeth. Because cameras have a nasty habit of finding them in close-ups, you can't even get away with amalgam in your back molars.

The other vital thing to know about amalgam fillings is that their major component (about 50%) is elemental mercury, which leaches into your tissues as your fillings degrade over the years. It may cheer you up to know that mercury is less poisonous than plutonium, but only just. Plutonium is the most toxic chemical element, and mercury is the next one on the list.

Heavy-metal poisoning is cumulative. Metals such as mercury, lead, arsenic and cadmium are unlikely to be naturally excreted from the body once they're in. And they accumulate. A little bit here adds to a little bit there, and as time passes, you find yourself subject to low-level mercury poisoning. The symptoms include chronic skin diseases, loss of energy, immune-system suppression, loss of memory, epilepsy and associated neurological disorders, allergies (such as hay fever), depression and chronic fatigue. Mercury shows a strong affinity to brain tissue. It accumulates in the pituitary gland, which has a major function in the regulation of emotions. Perhaps amalgam fillings aren't the best idea for performers?

Additionally, the constant presence of different metals in your mouth produces a weak electrolytic effect. The pH balance of saliva is fine if the mouth contains only tissue and teeth. The addition of mercury amalgam or gold fillings, or a metallic partial denture plate for a couple of lost teeth, provoke electrolytic conditions which promote corrosion of your amalgam fillings as well as affecting your whole metabolic balance. You turn into a sort of weak-output human battery.

Some dentists still use amalgam fillings, for two reasons:

1. They're cheaper than more stable filling materials. Dental work is always expensive, and patients can save by electing to use a cheaper filling material.
2. It's a lot easier for dentists to do fillings with amalgam. It takes less procedural care to prepare and insert. The amalgam is a more forgiving material, easier to manipulate and its setting time isn't so swift as some polymers. It demands less manual skill to shape and fill a dental cavity with amalgam.

For both cosmetic and health reasons, singers would be well advised to have any amalgam fillings removed and replaced with white, inert polymers, or similar, high-impact resins unlikely to have toxic effects or to upset the body's electrochemical balance.

Extractions

You create and enhance resonances within your voice by the unique shape of your dental arch: the semicircles formed by your upper and lower teeth. In particular, the shape of that curve in relation to your hard palate creates a unique sounding-board which, in part, accounts for the specific timbres of your individual sound. It's your vocal fingerprint, formed by the physics of your mouth cavity.

Think of the different shapes of hollow-body guitars. Think of the wooden resonating cases of a violin, a viola, a 'cello and a double bass. People's mouths differ just as radically. Hence, if you have teeth extracted, leaving holes in that arch of white bone, the sound profile will differ, and most probably for the worse. You'll have to compensate somehow, produce better resonating effects with different parts of your vocal tract. But be aware that the vocal tract is always a factor in the quality of sound you produce.

Prosthetics

Singing with bad false teeth is as useful as tapdancing with a wooden leg. Apart from offering comedians a swag of opportunities for hilarious sight gags, neither is a circumstance which a professional performer can countenance.

Your dentist must be skilled enough to know how to work within both the sound-producing and cosmetic requirements of your industry. Get yourself up to date with the latest information on the huge range of bridge structures designed for every conceivable eventuality and know when crowns are your best option. All this has a direct effect on your sound-production capabilities. Stay aware, and expect state-of-the-art updates from your dental professional.

Overcome that dental rot perpetuated by bad dentistry and skilled comedians. Find yourself a wonderful dentist, and enlist them as an ally in keeping and building your sound. And, to put the cost factor into perspective, ask any of your professional guitarist friends how much they spend on updating their amps and effects pedals. Singers have instrument maintenance costs too.

Skin

'You gotta have skin' parodied comedian Bob Newhart back in the 1960's. And it's more than a truism for performers. You can have a headache, asthma, arthritis, a pulled muscle, a whole lot of things plaguing you ... as long as you can cover their effects with a smile, long sleeves and trouser legs, you can still audition for work in many areas. But once the skin on your face has a paisley pattern to it, your future lies in voice-over and recording gigs — if you're lucky.

Anyone who hires performers, and anyone who works with people whose bodies need to be in good condition for their craft, can tell how well you are from the state of your skin. Your skin acts as a sort of printout of your body's general state of health. It is, in fact, the largest, single organ of your body. Ignore it at your peril.

Concern for your skin goes beyond the merely cosmetic. If you're getting by on junk food, too little sleep, too much tension and alcohol, and your skin erupts, you can hardly be surprised. But merely to apply a medicated ointment to fix your troubled skin is just like using a band-aid to treat leprosy.

Cold Sores

Some unfortunate performers have a tendency to get cold sores (herpes simplex virus) on their face just before an audition or a film shoot or a big concert. The herpes is triggered by nerves, and once the performers are anxious enough, bingo! The only way to break the cycle is to deal with your nerves. Hypnotherapy, acupuncture, a naturopath skilled in constitutional homoeopathy — here are three good ways to start sorting out anxiety responses. And there are many more therapeutic approaches if none of those does the trick. Don't accept cold sores as your inevitable fate.

Pimples

Distressing, and frequently impossible to conceal. If your skin eruptions are caused by the hormonal lucky-dip of adolescence, there is little that you can do except to adopt scrupulous face hygiene (fresh towels and face washers, careful cleansing) and steer clear of any foods which are likely to trigger a fresh outburst. You should already know what these are, because the cause-and-effect process with skin eruptions is pretty swift and dramatic.

If you have yet to work these connections out, start now. Keep a careful eye on your skin health. When it gets worse, work out what you have just eaten that differs from what you ate when it was all smooth and healthy. No matter how good a dermatologist you consult, you are best placed to be your own nutritional adviser by sorting out which foods are likeliest to trigger a skin eruption.

Performers who are well past adolescence but still collect a crop of pimples in production week probably don't need to be reminded that many skin conditions are triggered by stress. It may help to refer back to the 'Fixing Fear' section in Chapter 7, which offers an array of practical approaches to the management of anxiety.

Eczema and friends

The quick answer to eczema outbreaks is often that old stand-by, the topical corticosteroid. Yes, if you go to the doctor as soon as eczema recurs and get a prescription for your pet betamethasone, it sorts itself out after a couple of applications and you'll be fixed soon. No worries.

Pull the plug on this automatic sequence. Start finding out for your career's sake exactly *why* you get any of the multitude of variants of this distressing skin response. Yes, the magic ointment usually fixes it, but your body is yelling at you whenever it breaks out like this. Just for once, take a bit of time to listen to its message — you may well be surprised to find out that once you've discovered the basic cause(s) and fixed them up, you're infinitely healthier and happier all over. And, naturally, your skin will show it.

Eczema is another one of those disorders which often has stress as a root cause. As with cold sores (*see* above), you may find it useful to look at suggestions for anxiety management in the FIXING FEAR section of Chapter 7.

A PAIN IN THE NECK

I've known people to suffer head and neck pain on and off for years, employing nothing more than a shrug and a mild analgesic to manage their affliction. If this pain is caused by a dysfunction of your jaw joint (the temporo-mandibular joint), you'd be wise to make sure that its cause is remedied. Structural imbalances in the head and neck can impede your singing, let alone hurt a lot.

Interestingly, there are two areas of the body which don't self-correct bio-mechanically: the jaw joint and leg length discrepancies. In addition, these two systems are inter-related. Tension in the whole musculature of the head, neck and mouth is dependent to a large extent upon the bio-mechanics of the jaw joint and the length of the legs. If these are not in proper balance, then it will create tension in many of the muscles of the head and neck including that assortment of strap muscles at the front of the throat. All this obviously has a direct bearing on vocal folds, the floor of the mouth and tongue tension — hot spots of the singing performer's anatomy.

The problem is best tackled from both ends: a good dentist and a good podiatrist working in concert can re-establish balanced bio-mechanical relationships. Your reward is freedom from head and neck pain and more freedom in the jaw joint.

GOOD SPORTS

There are some sports which will actively assist your work as a singing performer, and there are some which are not all that useful. If you love sport, it's wise to play the ones that help your career while they divert and relax you. Remember, your body is your instrument and your profession demands that you are able to play it brilliantly and at short notice, without difficulty.

Sports that help build and strengthen upper torso musculature are best for singers. If your pectoral muscles are especially advantaged, so much the better. Aerobic exercise enhances circulation and helps build lung capacity. Look for sporting activities that build extra strength into the muscles of the lower back and lower abdomen: you'll need them as pivots to ensure the stability of your breathing technique.

Always do stretches and a physical warm-up before you start any sporting activity. Strap up any weak joints, especially if your health care professional has advised it.

Ball Games

Tennis is pretty useful for singers. It demands a flexible body, agility, speed and sharp reactions as well as an awareness of your body's own reactions. There's a nice workout for pecs and lats too. Always wear good sports shoes to minimise jarring to the knees and the likelihood of shin splints.

Beware of contact sports if you're in a production: the likelihood of injury soars when you have the chance of a basketballer or footballer barrelling into you. Hockey and lacrosse are less advisable ball sports for performers in the run of a production, while table tennis, which helps build rapid reflexes while keeping one's opponent out of harm's way, is somewhat better.

Cycling

Bicycle riding is a mixed blessing: it builds aerobic fitness, maintains flexibility in your legs, builds muscle and also gets you to places without the cost to the environment which the internal combustion engine demands of us. But if you're cycling in a reasonably built-up area, your nose and mouth are perfectly placed to collect the exhaust fumes of these engines.

Out in the countryside, bike riding is wonderful. If you're lucky enough to live and work in a city which has a good system of bike tracks apart from the main roads, then the bike is a great adjunct to maintaining your fitness.

If, however, you find yourself with sore, dry, itchy eyes, a nasty rasp to the voice and a feeling of tightness in the chest, consider whether you may be suffering from the effects of exhaust fumes. City bikers should wear a smog mask.

Martial Arts

Most martial arts, including aikido, kendo, judo, kung fu and karate, have a great accumulation of wisdom about body awareness. The discipline is challenging, the breath training is beneficial and the skills are often remarkably applicable to performance. Isolation exercises (working a specific muscle or muscle set whilst keeping adjacent musculature in as relaxed a state as possible) are a specific benefit, and the resultant flexibility and sharp reflexes can only advantage you as a performer.

Skipping

The equipment is cheap, and you don't have to join a club or pay admission. Get yourself a skipping rope, and skip anywhere. Beware of traumatising your knee joints by landing heavily or awkwardly. Always wear sports shoes to absorb the shock of landing, and try not to skip on concrete surfaces if you can help it.

Surfing and Wind-surfing

The combination of benefits offered by these sports is almost perfect for serious singers. You get solitude, sea breezes, a solid workout for your pecs, lats and abs, a sense of bodily freedom and a lot of moisture all round you.

Beat that. The possibility of injury from an awkwardly-twisted muscle or an anti-social marine creature is the only impediment.

Swimming

It stretches, it promotes flexibility, it builds aerobic fitness — and it does it all without letting you jar your body. Your whole weight is supported by the water as you exercise the parts of you which will best benefit your work as a singer. Who could ask for anything more?

If you want to work on consciously building up your lung capacity, try swimming underwater for increased periods of time. Your body is driven to seek and utilise the reserve oxygen it tucks away within its tissue. This process mimics the demands you make on your body in performance, when a sung phrase is hurtling towards the end of readily available breath.

Watch out for the drying effects of chlorine if you swim in a pool. Drink more water. Pool swimmers should also be aware of the probability of ear infections; ear plugs are the answer. Ocean swimming is preferable to pools: there are beneficial trace elements in sea water and you will often find that minor skin ailments respond favourably to a regular swim in the sea.

Tai Chi

This is a great sport, a great performance preparation, and a remarkably non-invasive exercise. Tai chi, done correctly, can only benefit your musculature, your reflexes and your discipline as a performer. It is also accessible and beneficial for people of any age. When an older performer has to hang up their tennis racket because their joints aren't up to it any more, tai chi remains as an all-round body toner and exercise of choice.

Walking

This is the cheapest and most accessible exercise imaginable. Walking builds both stamina and aerobic fitness while it takes you somewhere else for nothing. As with skipping, it is sensible to wear sports shoes which tend to absorb shock. It is far healthier to walk than to jog or run.

Jogging is not the best thing you can do for your body. Running or jogging, carelessly executed, can cause pulled muscles, strained tendons and plain grumpiness from all that discomfort you've put yourself through. Jogging also tends to degrade knee cartilage. If you must run or jog, only do it in really good sports shoes — they will help to minimise the shock to your legs. Additionally, try not to force a regimented pattern of breathing on yourself as you jog. It's counter-productive to the flexible pattern of breath which every singer needs.

Weight training

Circuit training is probably the best. Plenty of repetitions of small weight-loads is excellent, and is unlikely to compromise the health of your vocal folds.

Yoga

Yoga's combination of mental and physical disciplines encourages great body flexibility and enhanced breathing, whilst all the time giving you a gently consistent stretching workout. Yoga can provide perfect, regular toning for performers. A regular weekly yoga class, even at beginner level, will repay dividends.

A wise yoga instructor will never give beginners any exercise that places too much stress on their joints. Your yoga class should feel like a tonic for the body, not a marathon of screaming sinews and wrenched muscles.

CHAPTER 15

Friends and Enemies

Her teeth were yellow. Her bottom lip had begun to hang. It'd looked so good a few years ago when she could let it slip to a murderous pout that was rarely wasted. And her voice, she was going croaky. She didn't sound like Lauren Bacall anymore.

Tim Winton, *Cloudstreet*,
Penguin, Melbourne, 1991

What's good for my voice? What's going to hurt my voice? How can I make intelligent lifestyle choices that will help me in my work as a singing actor, a singing dancer, a singing musician, or a singer either in rock, pop, opera, recitals or a folk group? Here's a partial list of what's hot, together with background information, hints and explanations.

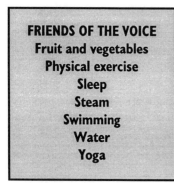

FRIENDS OF THE VOICE
Fruit and vegetables
Physical exercise
Sleep
Steam
Swimming
Water
Yoga

✓ *Fruit and Vegetables*

Uncooked fruit and vegetables are very easily digested. Your body always appreciates them. It is especially beneficial for you to eat raw fruit and vegetables when you are ill. You are fuelling your body's efforts to recover whilst giving it the least downtime in order to metabolise the food. It can then attend to its top-priority task, that of repairing and renewing itself.

Cooked vegetables still have a lot to be said for them, especially if they were organically grown and you cook them yourself.

Fruit and vegetable juices are of particular use to vocal performers: they have a high water content, contain minerals and trace elements which assist your body's tasks and offer a range of vitamins as well. Freshly juiced fruit and vegetables rate at the top of the list, but if you're on tour and have no kitchen facilities, commercial juices can help to maintain or restore your health.

✓ *Physical Exercise*

Refer to Chapter 14, 'A Body to Sing With' and Chapter 16, 'Keeping Healthy', which discuss the well-being of your instrument — the body.

Until singers openly admit to themselves the particularly physical nature of singing, their only hope is, at best, polite noises in the right key. That's not singing. Enjoy your body, work closely with it, become its trainer as well as its inhabitant. Sometimes, it's helpful to see your own body in dispassionate terms, as if viewing someone else's racehorse. Think about its health, its likely form and what sort of a wager you'd be prepared to place upon its performance. This is, of course, precisely the mode of thinking which any of your prospective employers will use.

No matter how heavenly your voice is, if your body lacks the stamina to carry you to the end of the opera, set or musical, then your lovely voice cannot be commercially heard.

✓ *Sleep*

Cheap, smart and ecologically sound. It does 'knit up the ravell'd sleave of care', just as Shakespeare said. I've had days when I felt like a very unravelled cardigan sleeve: a decent sleep has knitted up all the dropped stitches and I've bounced out of bed large as life and twice as objectionable.

Chemically assisted sleep is never as useful for your body as natural sleep. While you're off with the tranquilliser fairy, slowed down enough to sleep, your body's abilities to heal and repair itself are also slowed down, so you get less benefit from drug-aided sleep. It's better than nothing, but even a little sedative will still leave you feeling substandard.

✓ *Steam*

This is one of the singer's best friends. It's the low-cost, high-efficiency remedy for a tired voice, a dry voice, a stressed voice. You can never hurt anything by giving yourself a steam treatment, which is more than you can say for some remedies. An added advantage is that it's good for your skin too.

Steam-laden air is particularly soothing. Aren't there times when you let the hot shower run for longer than is strictly necessary just because you feel like the luxury of a steam-filled bathroom? How good it feels to sing in the billowing clouds of warm moisture! If ever you sense any restriction in your breathing, a steamy atmosphere will always ease it.

A steam treatment reproduces those good effects in a way that specifically helps your voice. Pour boiling water into a large bowl, hold your face over the steam and cover both your head and the bowl with a towel to ensure that your whole breathing environment is warm and steamy. Remember to take off your glasses or contact lenses.

Do this for *20 minutes*. Any less than that will not be long enough to do the trick. Get yourself comfortable before you start the process: put a good piece of music on the system, switch on your answer machine, set the bowl up in a place where you can sit comfortably. To help ease persistent coughing, try a steam treatment using a few drops of eucalyptus, thyme, or cypress oil in the boiling water. (Caution: use steam inhalations with care if you have asthma.)

✓ *Swimming*
Swimming offers freedom of movement and complete body support, allied with disciplined propulsion of the body — it's a top activity for singers (*see* Chapter 14, 'A Body to Sing With').

✓ *Water*
The world's surface is 70% water. This should tell us something about the physiology of the species that have adapted to its environment. Two molecules of hydrogen to one of oxygen is the basis of your physical existence. Water helps flush toxins from the cells of your body. If there's more water around, there's more chance of ridding yourself of toxic waste.

Singers need more water more often — our needs are greater than those of other mortals. Remember that it will take about 20 minutes for your body to absorb a drink of clear water. It cannot do you any active good until then, so it's a good idea to think ahead when you feel your throat drying out because of your surroundings.

There are problems as well as pleasures when you carry your instrument with you at all times. It means that you often have to think about work when everyone around you is thinking leisure. As you lie on the beach, enjoying a lazy day, or as you tramp through the wilderness on a bush-walking holiday, you still carry your instrument with you. Take a swig of water there and then. Water is cheap and it's socially acceptable to drink it at any time. Never leave home without it.

✓ *Yoga*
This is splendid for any performer: it builds body flexibility and enhances breathing. *See* Chapter 14, 'A Body to Sing With'.

ENEMIES OF THE VOICE

There are some things that singers should avoid. Some environments, some foods, some drugs and some activities can threaten the health and strength of your voice; it is wise to be aware of them

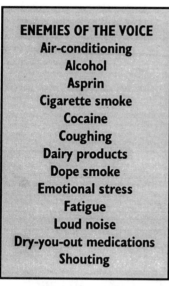

ENEMIES OF THE VOICE
Air-conditioning
Alcohol
Asprin
Cigarette smoke
Cocaine
Coughing
Dairy products
Dope smoke
Emotional stress
Fatigue
Loud noise
Dry-you-out medications
Shouting

✗ *Air-conditioning*

This is an insidious foe, and difficult to avoid. Air-conditioning not only dries out your throat but all of you. If you find yourself stranded in air-conditioned premises, drink inordinate amounts of water. If you're aware of what air-conditioning can do to you, it's possible to soldier on and perform in air-conditioning, although you'll become a bit waterlogged in the process.

✗ *Alcohol*

The major practical fact you need to know about alcohol is that it acts as a desiccant. It filches water from cells. If you question the truth of this, think back to a time when you had a goodly amount to drink. You went to sleep, then, later, woke up with a desperate thirst. Perhaps you went to the fridge and drank the best part of a two-litre carton of orange juice, then padded back to bed and slept. That's what alcohol does to you. So, if you have to use your voice tomorrow, it's sensible not to dehydrate your tissues tonight. And never, ever sing when you've just drunk alcohol. Your vocal equipment will be dried out, less flexible and more easily strained. *You* may feel well lubricated. Your throat is not. When you don't have to earn your money with your voice, you can go out drinking with your mates and sing the entire Black Sabbath back catalogue at your local karaoke.

✗ *Aspirin*

A potential danger for all voice users, aspirin has been positively linked to haemorrhage in the vocal fold areas. If you need an analgesic, check the tiny print on the label to make sure it contains no aspirin.

✗ *Cigarette Smoke*

Smoking is a handicap, much as high-performance racehorses carry lead in their saddle-bags in order to equalise race performances and thereby make the outcome more interesting.

Cigarette smoke sears the delicate mucous membranes in your larynx. As well, it stimulates your sinuses to produce far more mucus than is normal in order to protect those delicate membranes. Your whole vocal tract ends up coated with mucus. Perhaps your voice feels glugged up. It is.

All this is equally true for the non-smoker who performs in a smoke-filled room. When you sing, much more air gets drawn into your lungs than you normally need for simply existing, standing around and chatting. More air means more second-hand smoke. Even more unfairly, you inhale this smoke-laden air without the benefit of the filter that most of the first-time smokers used.

In order to justify their habit, some smokers like to list successful and famous singers who are also known to be smokers. Imagine how much more wonderful those performers would be if they *didn't* smoke. Are you happy to carry the same amount of lead in your saddle-bag as these famous performers do? Would you exceed them in talent and skill if you didn't smoke? Think about it.

If you want a comparison that has nothing to do with the emotive area of smoking, try this: let's pretend that a wonderful dancer whom you greatly admire has had to have cruciate ligaments removed in both knees because of injury. Their brilliant career still flourishes as they courageously continue to perform. Let's pretend further that you dream of being a top-flight dancer. Are you planning the surgical removal of both your cruciate ligaments in order to emulate your idol? Or are you setting yourself up for stardom with two physically sound, flexible and intact legs ... and giving the stars a run for their money?

Since you already know how bad for your general health smoking is, I guess you've thought through the logic of it all and decided that there's a future for amputees in showbusiness. Even if you can sing above the challenges that all the chemical constituents of cigarettes present to your throat and lungs, there are the circulation problems to deal with.

✗ Cocaine

Snorting coke removes the sensitivity you need to be able to operate your voice. It makes you feel good. Why? Because when you ingest cocaine, it renders your body's information system wholly unreliable and you haven't got a clue how you *really* are.

Cocaine works like a dentist's local anaesthetic injection, but without the needle. It induces massive mucus production as well (the typical coker's snivel). You can't feel your throat; you can't sense what your larynx is up to. And what your larynx does is to swell and become irritated, thereby losing its flexibility and accuracy.

You cannot perform on cocaine; you're likely to do irreparable damage to your voice and you certainly won't sound good while you're about it.

✗ Coughing

Coughing is one of the most abrasive things you can do to your vocal folds. In terms of duress and strain, a hacking cough does precisely that — to your vocal cords. So try not to, whatever the ailment. It's terribly tough on your voice.

A word of caution when choosing cough lozenges: never, ever place any work strain on your voice if you are using cough lozenges which have anaesthetic properties. You can tell which ones they are by the glowing promises printed on the packet. They promise they'll stop you feeling the pain of a sore throat. They do. You can't feel *anything* in your throat for a few hours. Imagine how much of a mess you can make of your voice when you can't feel what you're doing to it as you sing.

✗ Dairy Products

Some folk have more trouble with these delicious voice traps than others. However, the literature has long asserted that if anything's likely to trigger a good crop of mucus in anyone, it's likely to be this food group, or that other culprit, less suspected but just as frequently guilty — the potato. Dairy products therefore deserve your caution.

If you find that shortly after you've had any dairy product, your sinuses are crammed and your vocal resonance is negligible, perhaps you should turn your back on the whole food family: milk, cream, butter, cheese, yoghurt, ice-cream, milk chocolate.

There's always soy milk, which is, in my experience, unlikely to provoke any mucus excess. Goat's milk is fine for some folk, too. And there's always Vitari for ice-cream addicts.

Ensure that you supplement those parts of your diet which dairy products once provided, especially calcium. A prime source of calcium is raw sesame seeds, and parsley, almonds, sunflower seeds and camomile tea are all good calcium sources.

A reminder: calcium assimilates and functions best within the body when in conjunction with vitamins A, C and D, phosphorus and magnesium. Brewer's yeast and kelp provide useful sources for a combination of vitamins, minerals and trace elements.

✗ Dope Smoke (Cannabis sativa)

First up, I've neither time nor space for legal or moral arguments. Let's face it, a lot of good people use this social analgesic freely and cheerfully.

Here are the facts that matter to singing performers.

Cannabis burns hotter than tobacco, so its smoke hits your throat at a far higher temperature than that of cigarette smoke. It carries more resins and topical irritants within it than does cigarette smoke — more than ordinary tailor-mades or rollies, more than French cigarettes, even more than beedies. A good rule of thumb: one joint equals one pack of cigarettes.

Because of its combustion temperature, dope smoke tends to remove the lining off your throat tissues. It's rather like falling over and grazing your knee where the abrasion removes the top layer of your skin. A clear fluid (plasma) may ooze through the abrasion and it stings furiously, as surface wounds tend to do. Now imagine that tissue minus its top layer of skin and relocated in your throat. Try seeing your vocal folds weeping plasma. And never, ever again put your voice to any work at all for *at least* three clear days after smoking dope.

Now, the good news: it's the superior quality of the blood-circulation system to your head and neck. Have you observed how freely head wounds bleed? You'll lose far more blood from a cut on your head than from the same kind of cut to your leg or hand because there are more blood vessels in your head and neck than in any other part of your body. As a result, head and neck wounds tend to heal much faster than similar wounds elsewhere.

Because of all this, it should take only *three clear days* for your damaged throat tissue to repair itself. That's 72 hours. If you had a joint on Saturday, it's not automatically true that you can sing again on Tuesday. For instance, if you had a smoke on Saturday night at 11 pm, you might be clear for a Wednesday morning rehearsal and you should be absolutely all right for a Wednesday night performance. Because your three clear days only takes you to 11 pm Tuesday night.

No bong is able to lower the temperature of the smoke sufficiently to stop it burning your skin; it cannot render dope smoke harmless to your throat. Neither an Arabian hookah pipe nor any number of ingenious filters will prevent surface burns to your throat tissue.

✗ Emotional Stress

Personal distress can wreck the health of your body. It will tighten all the muscles around your neck and shoulders. It will give extra work to your nervous system. It will play havoc with your digestion, and turn your last meal to quick-setting concrete.

Performance requires free availability of toned, relaxed muscles ready to work at split-second command, and a calm control of your nervous responses so that you can give the performance all your emotional attention.

If it's at all possible, avoid any emotional stress before performance. If you feel nervous, edgy and argumentative, stick pins in a teddy bear, or do knitting or crossword puzzles before you perform — whatever helps you to relax. Avoid confrontation: it bleeds you of performance energy. If necessary, promise yourself a huge blow-up argument after the show. Never, ever before. It short-changes your audience.

✗ Fatigue

Fatigue is a dangerous condition in which to work. You become less likely to exercise vigilance in performance, and that's when accidents can happen.

I can hear tiredness in a voice, and it's an insult to your audience for you to offer it a vocal performance with that weary, raspy edge to it. If you're performing, get sufficient rest to ensure your performances are up to scratch.

✗ Loud Noise

If you subject yourself to inordinately loud sound, you will throw your pitch sensitivity out of balance. Don't go to a rock concert tonight and try to do a voice-over tomorrow morning. Your ear will be out. Don't turn up to rehearsals for a music-theatre piece the morning after head-bangers' night out. You won't be able to spot your vocal line, let alone sing it with any accuracy.

Loud noise mashes the nerve endings of your aural acuity. Always wear semi-permeable ear-plugs when you go to a concert that you suspect might pump out a solid barrage of sound. You'll still hear the music. These special ear-plugs, designed for musicians who need to hear their music accurately but must protect their hearing from harmful, high-intensity frequencies, are available from chemists. They're not cheap, but they last for a very long time and are an essential tool of trade.

Even with your ear-plugs in place, don't forget that all that sound is bound to have a fair impact on your finely tuned biofeedback system. Give your neurons time to mend before you expect them to do the highly accurate work that singing demands.

✗ Dry-you-out and other Medications
Dry-you-out Medications: You've got a runny nose, a bad dose of hay fever, the 'flu. You hit the anti-histamines and the pseudo-ephedrine-based pills: medications such as Actifed, Demazin and Telfast, designed to decrease the production of excess mucus in the upper respiratory tract. If you've got a permanently sniffy nose, or you can feel a steady nasal drip, these are the sorts of drugs you'd be likely to take. They will frequently halt the sniffles and unblock the mucous glug. Unfortunately they dry out *everything*.

All the tissue that has anything to do with vocal production is moist tissue. It relies on a continuous supply of water to its cells in order to function. You cannot sing on a dried-out set of vocal folds, because they lack elasticity. Imagine your vocal folds as a pair of squishy, stretchy rubber bands. When you want to sing high, they get pulled out longer and skinnier; as your voice goes low, they get fatter and slacker. Now imagine perished rubber which has lost its elasticity. Dried-out and cracked, it snaps when you put any pressure on it. So do your vocal folds.

Other Medications: As a useful rule of thumb, presume that most medications will have some effect on your voice quality. Even if your doctor is writing you a prescription for a medical condition that isn't remotely connected with your voice, always ask first, 'What effect will this medication have on my voice?'

For example, unwelcome vocal side-effects are likely from some blood pressure tablets, beta-blockers (often prescribed to help nervous performers deal with stage fright), sleeping pills and hormonal medications.

✗ Shouting
No, not even in indignation or distress. Here, the insidious enemy is pleasure. Cheering for your sporting team, hooting and hollering at a party (especially if you've been drinking alcohol, which dries out your voice), yelling at a rock concert — all of this takes a toll on your voice, especially if you scrape and screech away at your poor vocal folds with less than considerate care.

CHAPTER 16

Keeping Healthy

He begins to sing again, softly, like the humming of a bee, then the
words shape on his lips and he breaks off.
"You know that song, son."
"Suppose I heard it somewhere before," I say.
"You dream it," he says. "It belong your country."
"I haven't got a country," I say. "I don't belong anywhere."
"You can't lose it," he says. "You go away but you keep it here." He
claps his hands under his ribs. "Inside. You dream that place and that
song too. I hear you sing it in your sleep."

Mudrooroo, Wild Cat Falling,
Angus & Robertson, Sydney, 1965.

All over the world, in every musical form imaginable, professional performers are singing wonderfully whilst ill, distressed or in pain. Their back may be killing them from a wrenched muscle in last night's show. They may have the mother of all head colds. One of their children may be in hospital, battling a life-threatening disease. Their long-term partner may have just walked out on them. And their audiences must never, ever know, or guess.

Literally millions of dollars are at risk if a top-line performer cancels. Even in shows where there are understudies, entrepreneurs know that ticket sales are badly affected if the big-name drawcards are erratic in their appearances. The understudy might be better than the 'name' star, but that's not who people come to see.

> **Healthy body, healthy mind, healthy spirit.**

What happens when word gets round that the star everyone is lining up for may or may not be on when they get to the show? Your employer and mine, the general public, loses confidence in the worth of that high-priced ticket. Box office goes down the drain. The star's name becomes coupled with that kiss-of-death descriptor 'unreliable'. When the trade starts describing you thus, get cracking on writing your memoirs. It'll be the only reliable source of income for you in the future.

Does all this sound a bit too heartless for you? Do you find yourself asking: how can artists tolerate this callous disregard for their physical and emotional health? Where's the humanness and sensitivity with which any management of a performance piece should treat its performers? The answer is: in the producer's wallet. And rightly so. Look at it from your *real* employer's point of view, your audience.

The person who buys a ticket to see your concert, musical, opera or recital pays a fixed amount of money to see any one of your shows in the run. What if your customer happens to turn up on a night when you feel miserable, ill or angry, and your illness or distress affects the quality of the show? They get less of a show for their money.

Much of the discipline of performance involves telling yourselves creative lies. My father, no mean singer himself, used to say the task resembles conning yourself up a wattle tree and selling yourself a ladder to get down.

Set art to one side when you think about our trade, and try to see your work as that of a skilled tradesperson, whose reliability and expertise are the reason they're hired again and again.

In order to work at this level of energy output, you have to be intensely healthy. Not just the jog-round-the-block sort of health, but healthy in your eating, sleeping, practising, body-toning and mental attitudes. And with a healthy spirit too.

I Don't Feel 100 Per Cent

Here are a few useful rules to optimise your well-being when you feel less than marvellous, for whatever reason.

Eat Less Meat

The extra work your body has to put into metabolising the complex components of meat could be more usefully directed towards making your body feel better. Whatever's wrong with you, your body is keen to fix it. It wants to be well even more than you do; it's built that way. But if you're fuelling your system with food which takes a fair bit of energy to digest and assimilate, then the repair system of your body hasn't sufficient staffing levels to fix you as well.

Eat More Raw Food

Try to have fewer cooked foods. There's no need to be fanatical about it, but as a rule, the less processed the food is, the happier your body is to take it on board. When you feel under par, it's smart to humour your body; you can't go on stage without it.

Drink More Water

When in doubt, drink more water. You can't go wrong and you're unlikely to overdose.

Give Yourself a Half-hour Holiday

Even a frantically busy person whose every waking moment is spoken for can take a half-hour holiday. Plan a half-hour of the day when you aren't needed by another soul in the universe, and, in the spirit of true selfishness, work out what you'd like to do just to cheer yourself up.

It needn't cost money, but it may cost time in planning and execution. Get up earlier; go to bed later; cancel a luncheon or dinner appointment you really didn't want to fulfil anyway; chisel that half-hour from the sheer cliff-face of your responsibilities.

Take a bath, read a trashy novel, sip coffee in a good café, have a full body massage, drive to the beach and go for an aimless saunter along the sand.

The emphasis here is on solitary non-productivity. You can be cheerfully irresponsible, unanswerable to a soul and do something just for yourself alone.

MENSTRUATION

When it's 'that time of the month' (or whatever your euphemism is), different parts of your body usually feel a bit bloated and uncomfortable, including your vocal folds.

When your vocal folds distend because of the hormonal cycle, you will probably sense a reduced range and a lack of flexibility. This is because the thicker vocal folds can't move around as freely as in their normally less-distended state.

Moral: be aware of your menstrual cycle and work with it. It's neither an illness nor a disability. Your body is healthy and fertile (whether you want to breed or not, it's ready and willing to). This cannot be all bad news. One of my friends is a blues singer, and she vows that she sings better when she has her period. When working your voice in the days before you expect your period to occur, try to feature flexibility exercises and light vocal patterns that extend the upper and lower range.

ALLERGIES

Don't keep excusing your vocal limitations with the old stock phrase, 'Of course, I'm a bit allergic, which unfortunately hinders my voice'. Start trying to find out what you're allergic to, and stop eating it, drinking it, wearing it or breathing it, if that's at all possible.

Recurrent allergies which pester your upper respiratory tract will trigger colds. You're then stuck with all *that,* as well as the original allergy.

A serious singer has to know how to keep well. Get your GP to refer you to a specialist in allergies. Tests may reveal what causes your allergic response. If you're all better once you remove the allergy-causing substance(s) from your house and life, then all's well and you're home free.

Sometimes, it takes more than one consultation with an allergy specialist to pinpoint the problem and then take remedial action. Be patient, be persistent and remember that when you walk out of the doctor's door, that doctor doesn't feel a thing if you don't get better. It's your body, your life and your professional future that bear the burden of that illness.

By way of alleviating the irritation and distress of allergies, consider homoeopathic remedies before your standard anti-histamine scrip which many a general practitioner will quickly write for you. The drying nature of these pharmaceuticals creates an adverse environment for your vocal cords (*see* Chapter 15, 'Friends and Enemies').

The names of good homoeopathic practitioners and naturopaths are often passed on from performer to performer in any given area. There's usually a singers' grapevine which will get you in touch with who's who of these life-saving practitioners.

ALTERNATIVE THERAPIES

These non-invasive methods are elegant and civilised therapies which come recommended by many centuries of continuous use. Many performers find so-called alternative therapies a useful option for maintaining health. When administered by skilled practitioners, these holistic procedures are a non-invasive way of fixing you up by refocusing your body's own resources rather than by depositing an array of extra chemical substances in your body.

Here is a list of some of the more readily available natural therapies:

Acupuncture

In this method, body energies are simply redirected in order to help your body to fix itself, which it frequently does. A lot of people who think they know all about this will tell you with relish that you get great big needles stuck into you. Shock. Horror. If you've undergone acupuncture treatment from a skilled practitioner, you will know that this is not the full story. Acupuncture is often intensely pleasant, relaxing and invigorating.

Diagnosis is mostly by the traditional Chinese method of reading the pulse. Just by feeling your wrist pulse with their fingers, good acupuncturists learn a great deal. Very fine needles are inserted into specific areas of your body. These will act rather like traffic signals to your body's energy, redirecting it from the healthy areas so that injured or ailing parts get extra blood flow, neural activity or whatever is needed.

Do the needles hurt? I have never felt pain from any acupuncture treatment. Lying on a table with fine filaments of silver sticking out of parts of me, I probably look like a half-finished porcupine. I snooze, I relax, I feel absolutely fine. And I'm no masochist, believe me.

Bach Flower Remedies

Related to homoeopathy, these gentle but remarkably effective remedies are designed to treat the emotional states underlying a range of illnesses. The original work was developed by British physician, pathologist, immunologist and bacteriologist Edward Bach. He came to view illness as a disharmony between body and mind, with symptoms as the external expression of negative emotional states.

Bach's research located thirty-eight plants with specific therapeutic use for particular problems. Essences distilled from the flowers of these plants are used by therapists trained in Bach Flower treatment. Current research has extended Bach's work to a far broader range of flowers, there are now specific Australian bush flower remedies, and even shell essences designed to work within Bach's principles.

Homoeopathy

This method is based on the opposite of 'A little of what you fancy does you good'. Micro-quantities of the active principle of whatever ails you are administered, and your body works out a game plan for fighting its foes from these introduced minute doses. Once your immune system has solved the problem, it can get to work on the macro-sized problem, using its own developed resources.

Hypnotherapy

Hypnotherapy is often a treatment of choice for actors, because their training has prepared them to use imagination in practical ways. As practised by a suitably qualified practitioner, hypnotherapy has an impressively broad range of applications. It is now becoming more common to find that psychologists and general practitioners have obtained specialist training in hypnotherapy.

Kinesiology

This is a system for achieving balance in the movement and interaction of a person's energy systems. If blocks and imbalances seem to be impairing physical, emotional or energetic well-being, muscle responses are gently tested to identify factors which may be contributing to such imbalances. Reflex and acupressure points are then used to stimulate the body's natural healing responses. These, used in conjunction with specific body movements and nutritional support, can help alleviate a remarkable range of problems.

Massage Therapies

There are a number of highly useful massage-based therapies, including:

Aromatherapy

This method, which is much more than nice smells, involves inhaling essential oils or massaging them into the skin. Specialist applications include stress management, skin disorders and pain management.

Reflexology

According to this method, each body area is represented on the soles of the feet, which are examined to diagnose dysfunction. The underlying principle is similar to acupressure or shiatsu. Treatment consists of highly specific foot massage and manipulation.

Reiki

This is healing through the hands. A reiki practitioner lays their hands on you and redistributes the energy fields within and around your body.

Rolfing

Rolfing involves connective tissue manipulation, which removes stress from the deeper level of muscles, thus restoring flexibility, balance and free movement to the body.

Shiatsu

This is rather like acupuncture without the needles. The principles of meridians applies, and vital spots in your body get deep, highly localised massage in order to re-route energies and help your body heal itself. It is also known as acupressure.

Naturopathy

This method takes a broad approach to the effective use of traditional natural health procedures. At its foundation, naturopathy believes that your body has an in-built tendency to be well, and that its inherent energies can be harnessed to fix itself up whenever it becomes ill. A practitioner who describes themselves as a naturopath, whatever their range of training and expertise, should always use procedures which treat the whole person.

A good naturopath should use an assortment of approaches towards healing and health: these will probably include herbal and homoeopathic preparations, acupuncture, nutritional counselling and nutritional supplements, massage and muscle balancing. Because of their eclectic skill base, a good naturopath is a gem of great price.

THE HEART AND THE MIND

Here's where most health issues start and finish. If you're bitter, distressed, fearful, rejected or grief-stricken, you are not healthy in your spirit. Your heart has an ailment. It is called emotional trauma.

Far from singing with the neat little flaps of tissue inside your neck, you truly sing with your heart and your head. The larynx decodes the brain's neural signals, and your brain only transmits them because your spirit (your heart? your soul? your inherently non-corporeal being?) is alive, well and actively interested in expressing itself.

A Bit of Zen

Imbedded within the wisdom of Zen Buddhism is a concept which the Japanese call *shin-gi-tai* . This means *Mind — Technique — Body*. Zen says that when each of these three elements is developed equally within a pupil, then they will enjoy success in defeating the crocodiles of their inner life: the anger, the ego, the lack of focus, the fears.

Special emphasis is placed upon the importance of training and developing the mind. Zen clearly warns that those pupils who choose to develop only their body and their technique will become victims of their own savage egos.

All performers need to keep working at their *body*-based skills; frequently, they will achieve this by using conscious *training* techniques. The supremely practical Zen masters remind you that it is also your duty to attend to the training of your *mind*. And when they say 'mind', they mean a great deal more than mere intellect.

To explain ... perhaps. In the Rinzai sect of Zen Buddhism, they often supply followers who are to engage in zazen (seated meditation) with a koan — a little puzzle solved by the intellect. As the pupil meditates on the illogical, zany koan they learn that in solving the riddle, one must strip away the restless mind, and come to rest in what Buddhists term the Void; the emptiness of Not Knowing. Maybe this is an old Eastern variant on Ignorance is Bliss.

Within the Void, one may hope to become the question. When you become the question, you also become the source. Once you become the source, you're home free. If you get the idea.

Zen teaching enables you to use your intuition to confront yourself; this gives you the power to discover and then unlock your true nature.

Surviving Bad News

What happens when you are notified of a tragedy this afternoon and you have to perform tonight? Any performer will tell you it can happen to you. Wise performers learn the faculty of setting their own woes aside for a while in order to perform, a process that takes experience and courage.

You commence by openly acknowledging to yourself that you feel like death on a stick. Your life is a mess. You have a gaping wound in your heart. Your self-esteem is going through the floor. Whatever the trouble, tell yourself bluntly and explicitly just how things are with you. *Deny nothing.* Don't force a cheery grin onto your tear-stained face. Tell yourself honestly how you feel.

The next stage involves your recognising that anything this bad needs serious time devoted to it. It demands, by its very immensity, your whole attention. This problem probably should not even be considered in certain places or in front of certain people. Perhaps you have a picture in your mind of the place and circumstances in which you could best start to try and make sense of this trouble or tragedy. Sitting in a hot bath with a bottle of vodka? Lying on a deserted summer beach at midnight? Going for a ten-kilometre bike ride? Having coffee with your closest friend and telling them all about it?

Dancing in the loudest disco you can find with a horde of weird strangers who all ignore you?

Any preferred scenario is unlikely to bear any resemblance to what goes on backstage before you have to perform ... so proceed to stage three. Pick this trouble of yours up carefully, preferably using tongs and wearing protective clothing on your spirit. Gently deposit it in a waiting box, a box within your heart and/or mind where it will become neither less nor more than what it is now, but will wait with integrity until you can deal with the hugeness of its distress honestly and satisfactorily.

Now you are free to perform. Your trouble is stored, insulated, safely away from your working mind. There is no point in denying your distress; nor should you ever belittle it to yourself. If you can't deal candidly with yourself, you're unlikely to manage it with others.

CHAPTER 17

The Singing Asthmatic

(Written in collaboration with Dr David Mitchell)

Anyone who has worked around professional performers knows that in many a make-up case you'll find a little plastic puffer ... just in case of an asthma attack. We have no official statistics to support this, but our observation in working with musicians, dancers, singers and actors over a period of years is that the entertainment industry probably has a higher-than-national average incidence of asthma amongst its workers.

The lead singer in the last musical you saw; the prima ballerina in the last ballet you went to; that madcap actor in the last slapstick comedy you enjoyed — each one of them may well have been prone to asthma.

Learning to *manage* asthma is the trick. Once you understand what it is, how you get it and what measures you may sensibly take to prevent it or to limit its effects, then you're well on the way to being able to work despite asthma. This saves you from having to limit your performance repertoire to tatty reruns of the last act of *La Traviata*.

Both conventional and alternative approaches to the treatment of asthma continue to offer innovations in treatment. And there's more to the management of asthma than reclining artistically on your divan and gasping 'Call the doctor!' There's a lot you can do for yourself. Below are a number of high-ingenuity, low-cost, do-it-yourself commonsense approaches to asthma therapy. Today's asthmatic performers can now live a full and active working life.

WHAT IS ASTHMA?

Asthma develops when the bronchial tubes become hypersensitive or overreactive. The bronchial tubes (bronchi) are the tubes which lead from your windpipe (trachea) to your lungs. This overreactive condition causes spasm or narrowing of the tubes, which limits your access to oxygen.

Remember, *asthma is a symptom, not a disease*. Asthma is usually triggered by something, so rather than automatically reaching for your puffer as soon as you feel that tell-tale raspy breathing, it makes sense for you to:

1 learn what that trigger is, and
2 try to avoid that trigger or prevent it from happening.

HOW DO YOU GET ASTHMA?

You can inherit it. You can get it after a severe chest infection. You can get it as a consequence of being exposed to toxic chemicals, either with or without fumes.

It is good common sense to attempt to identify the factor or factors which trigger the onset of your asthma. If you have been the subject of asthma attacks for a while, you will probably have very little trouble in identifying what's likely to set you off.

Precipitating factors (triggers) may include:

1 Infection
2 Allergy: dust; dust mites; pollens; moulds; horses, dogs, cats; chemicals, including aspirin and sulfa preservatives; foods (either allergy or intolerance)
3 Seasonal changes
4 Stress
5 Exercise: running, jumping, singing, dancing
6 Dehydration can bring on asthma even before exercise, and make exercise-induced asthma worse.

Your top priority is, of course, to find out what is likely to trigger the onset of asthma for you. Once you know this, devising cunning ways of controlling or avoiding these factors will markedly lessen the probability of asthma. There are a number of ways to determine what triggers asthma:

1 Skin tests
2 IgE and RAST blood tests. (Immunoglobulin E [IgE] is the antibody secreted in large amounts in an allergic reaction. The RAST blood test is specific for food and other allergies.)
3 Blood test for *Chlamydia pneumoniae* immunoglobulins.
4 Food elimination testing
5 Keeping a diary of when asthma occurs to see if there are common precursors to each event.

If, despite your every preventive measure, you still get asthma — what can you do? Today's asthmatics have access to a wide range of both preventative and therapeutic medication as well as complementary approaches to asthma treatment.

THE MEDICAL APPROACH

Prevention
Reduce the hypersensitivity with Intal or Intal Forte (sodium cromoglycate) or with more recently released Tilade (nedocromil), which is considered to be more potent than Intal. These widely used pharmaceuticals work by

preventing the allergy cells from releasing the histamine and other chemicals that cause the narrowing of the bronchial tubes.

They are *preventative*, or prophylactic, drugs. This means that it must be in your system *before* the asthma starts. Both Intal and Tilade may be taken for long periods of time without any problems. It's sensible to give yourself a top-up dose before you begin exercise, a dance class, a singing lesson and so on.

Treatment

1 *Reduce the inflammation*: When you have asthma, there will always be inflammation present in your bronchial tubes. Cortisone can be used to reduce this swelling. Injections or oral doses of cortisone used to be given for asthma, but it was found that these can cause serious side effects if taken for any length of time. If high doses were needed the patient had to wean off the cortisone very slowly. Nowadays pulse therapy (high dose for 3 or 4 days) obviates the need for weaning down from cortisone intake. There are now a number of safer, effective, low-dose cortisone sprays or puffers such as Pulmicort, Becotide and Aldecin. These deliver a small dose directly into and onto the lining of the bronchial tubes. Main side effect is oral thrush.

Inhaled steriods are a preventative and must be taken regularly. If an asthma attack has already commenced, you will need to *first* use a bronchodilator (*see* below) before puffing on one of your cortisone sprays. Once your bronchial tubes have been opened up, they can permit the inhaled cortisone to penetrate sufficiently deeply to reduce the inflammation. Just using the cortisone spray is an inefficient approach.

Recently, a new class of inhaled bronchodilators, the beta-agonists such as Serevent and Oxis/Foradile (same chemical, different delivery system) have become popular because they offer up to 12 hours' protection.

2 *Block the Immune Chemicals*: An exciting new development in asthma treatment is a once-daily tablet called Singulair (Montelukart). This chemical blocks the effect of leukotriene, an immune chemical released by white blood cells which causes bronchospasm/asthma. It appears to work as both a bronchodilator and an anti-inflammatory agent.

3 *Remove the infection*: Recently research around the world has implicated a bacterium called *Chlamydia pneumonias* as both a cause and a trigger for asthma. A blood test for immunoglobulins specific for *C. pneumoniae* can be done. If it is positive, then a two month course of Rulide 300mg once daily can eradicate this bacterium and decrease and/or remove the asthma.

4 *Open up the tubes*: Bronchodilators are used to relax and expand spasming, narrowed bronchial tubes. It is no coincidence that they are the most frequently used, abused and overused asthma drugs. Some say their overuse can lead to dependence. Bronchodilators such as Ventolin and Bricanyl provide a tremendously handy quick fix for opening up the bronchial tubes. Their effect can last for four to six hours. A new class of inhaled bronchodilators, the beta-agonists such as Servent and Oxis/Foradile are being used more and more. Why? Because their effect lasts up to 12 hours, making them ideal for

nocturnal cough, early morning wheeze/cough and as a longer protection against exercise asthma. Side effects of both groups of bronchodilators include tremors (shakes), fast pulse/heart rate, hyperactivity and dry mouth/throat.
5 *Severe cases*: These may require the use of the above drugs in a nebuliser, a machine which breaks liquid up into tiny droplets. The fluid therefore presents a larger surface area to the lungs, with beneficial effect. The liquid used is a mixture of saline and a chemical which positively affects lungs such as a bronchodilator or cortisone.

What's Best?

Nowadays, the best approach is a maintenance dose of Intal or inhaled steroid, with added bronchodilator as needed.

COMPLEMENTARY APPROACHES

It is important to acknowledge that complementary therapies and techniques might never replace conventional medicines in acute asthma. However, in the case of many individuals, they have been effective in reducing the number and the severity of attacks, as well as reducing the amount of medication needed.

Many of these therapies approach the asthma not as a separate problem but as part of a disturbed/malfunctioning body-mind-immune system within an individual. Such holistic treatment tends to be slower to exhibit measurable results; nor is it certain to always avert an acute attack. The sensible way to view these very useful therapies is as part of the whole range of treatment options.

1 Acupuncture by a skilled acupuncturist (*see* Chapter 16).
2 Homoeopathy (*see* Chapter 16)
 a. Consult a homoeopathy practitioner, or a Bio-energetic practitioner who uses Vega/Mora/Voll machines. (Bioenergetics, first discovered by Prof. Yokio Nakatani in 1950, incorporates the use of various instruments to measure the fluctuation in tiny electrical currents which flow through the myelin sheaths which surround the nerves. These pathways seem to match up with the acupuncture meridians or channels. Dr Reinhold Voll, a German physician and acupuncturist, discovered that there was a consistent correlation between charged electrical readings and an internal dysfunction of that acupuncture organ system.)
 b. Do it yourself, with the use of Brauer's Asthmaplex or Asthminplant from your health-food store.
3 Kinesiology (EK) / Touch For Health balancing: This is valuable therapy which can really help (*see* Chapter 16). Try a simple, do-it-yourself balancing process:
 a. Press hard with finger in the solar plexus (immediately below the point where your breastbone (sternum) and ribs meet, for approximately 30 seconds.

b. Tap your breastbone (sternum) eight to ten times at a point where the second button on your shirt is.

4 Meditation, relaxation: Fear, stress and anxiety can cause spasm in the bronchial muscles. Tension is contagious, and the muscles of the chest wall, diaphragm and neck are quick to catch it from the bronchi. Clearing the mind and the heart of conscious anxieties by a program of meditation or relaxation exercises is a useful means of creating a little extra space within your body has more of a chance to heal itself (*see* Chapter 16).

5 Hypnotherapy and self-hypnosis (*see* Chapter 16).

6 Buteyko breathing method: This new breathing technique, developed by the Russian doctor Professor Konstantin Pavlovich Buteyko, shows promising results. It consists of a training program that teaches asthmatics how to re-condition their breathing. Courses are held in each state, and are frequently advertised in major city newspapers.

7 Get rid of the cat/dog/horse: But try a poodle — their woolly fur is less allergenic.

8 Food: Avoid obvious food allergens: for example, milk, potatoes, sulphur on fresh, young wines.

9 Stop smoking.

10 Supplements

a. Zinc provides a protective lining to the bronchial tubes. A sign of zinc deficiency is white spots on fingernails. As zinc deficiency is very common, asthmatics can be helped by taking 220mg Zinc Chelate once daily.

b. Magnesium: although its mechanism is unknown, magnesium supplements help prevent/reduce the severity of asthma. Take 500mg elemental magnesium daily.

c. Vitamin C helps degrade (break down faster) histamine, one of the allergy chemicals that cause bronchospasm/asthma. Take 2000mg daily.

11 Coffee: strong black espresso, percolated or plunger coffee can open up the bronchial tubes and increase concentration. Too much can cause dry mouth, palpitation, sweating and the shakes, so go carefully. Never use instant coffee.

CHAPTER 18

Help! I Think I'm Getting a Cold

H elp! I think I'm getting a cold' is a cry from the heart that every singer utters at some time in their career. Everyone whose livelihood depends on their vocal quality becomes at least a little anxious at the threat of infection to their respiratory tract. Although well-trained actors and singers will frequently be able to perform whilst suffering from a cold, the full glory of their voice is unlikely to be heard. Singers have to work far harder than usual to sing on top of a cold whilst ensuring that their audience doesn't feel short-changed.

THE COMMON COLD

The common cold is anything but common. What we call 'a cold' is really one or more of an army of diseases caused by at least 80 and sometimes up to 200 viruses. This is why it's difficult to build immunity to the resultant illnesses and tough to find a cure.

Researchers worldwide continue in their quest for the medical holy grail — a cure for the common cold. Ready availability of a wonder drug is, however, still a long way down the track. Until all the trials and tests are completed, expect to see the usual displays at your local pharmacy: expectorants and cough suppressants, decongestants and anti-histamines.

While these over-the-counter remedies and palliatives will often help, there are some simple steps you can take in order to protect yourself from the possibility of catching a cold. The human body is a well-designed unit, built to combat viruses. If you happen to get a cold despite all your best efforts, there are some practical things you can do to minimise the worst effects of it.

Prevention
- Avoid stress: it makes people more susceptible to colds. Stress uses up your body's vitamins, thus causing alterations in the fine balance of micro-organism populations.
- Avoid other people with colds. Most importantly, try to avoid the kind of crowded, airtight environments that viruses thrive in, such as schools, cinemas and all forms of public transport.
- If it is impossible to avoid other people with colds, try to breathe only through your mouth for a while if someone near you coughs or sneezes.

Cold viruses usually prefer to enter the body through the nose.

- Take plenty of vitamin C. The human body cannot manufacture its own supply of this vitamin, so it will be grateful of the input. The body cannot store vitamin C for more than a day either, so it's sensible to include foods rich in this vitamin in your daily diet. Good sources of vitamin C include parsley, alfalfa sprouts, grapes, green peppers, berry fruits, raisins and blackcurrants. Most fresh fruits and all green vegetables contain some vitamin C.
- When you need to encourage your body to repel threatening infections, you can boost your immune system promptly in five ways:

1 Vitamin C powder (ascorbic acid *as* sodium ascorbate) 1 tablespoon twice daily.
2 Take the juice of two lemons and three cloves of fresh pressed garlic, with a little water.
3 Sleep.
4 Avoid negative thoughts and emotions.
5 Avoid food; the less you eat, the better.

DAMAGE CONTROL

To Fight Infection

- *Garlic* contains natural antibiotics and many other substances which can help fight infection. It's best in the raw: peel and chop a clove and eat it in a sandwich. Alternatively, make a drink with hot water, lemon juice, pressed garlic juice and some honey. For sore throats, nasty tonsils and the like, this is a front-line treatment.

- *Vitamin A* will improve the health of mucous membranes, fight the infection and boost your immune system all at the same time. Good sources for vitamin A include carrots and carrot juice, green leafy vegetables, pumpkins, mangoes, apricots, peaches, papayas, sweet potatoes, cantaloupes, bananas, lemon and orange peel, tomatoes, avocados, sunflower seeds, saffron, chillies, cayenne, paprika, kelp, fish oils, some dairy foods. Vitamin A is *destroyed* by cigarette smoking, heavy alcohol intake, preservatives in processed food and clear bottles that allow light through to their contents.

Note 1: If you need to take cortisone or the contraceptive pill, you should be aware that these medications interfere greatly with the body's ability to absorb vitamin A.

Note 2: Diabetics cannot convert carotene into vitamin A; a diabetic's best source of vitamin A is cod-liver oil.

To Shorten the Duration of a Cold

Echinacea is a natural plant extract that enhances the function of the immune system. It's available in pill or liquid form from health-food shops and some chemists, and it's safe for children. Take it in large doses every three or so hours to shorten the duration of a cold.

Take plenty of *vitamin C*. Mega-doses of vitamin C can help reduce the length of a cold and the severity of symptoms. This vitamin is used in so many metabolic pathways (more than 200) that you can't help but cheer your body up by offering plentiful supplies of vitamin C. The best way to take supplemental vitamin C is as a powder, preferably as sodium ascorbate, a more alkaline form of the vitamin. Always rinse your mouth out with clear water after taking vitamin C powder to prevent acidic attack on your teeth.

To Boost Your Immune System

Chillies are rich in immune-protective vitamins. They also stimulate chemical receptors in the mouth, which then cause a reaction in the mucous membranes, making your nose run and clearing stuffiness. Fresh horseradish, if available, has much the same effect.

To Re-hydrate Your System

Drink plenty of *fluids*. Recent research indicates that moderate alcohol consumption may help build resistance to the common cold, although you'll undo any benefit if you smoke as well. Alcohol is not an option before performances, however, because of its desiccant properties (*see* Chapter 15, 'Friends and Enemies'). Water and fruit juice are much more traditional and healthy ways of soothing sore throats and preventing your sinuses from drying out.

To Aid Fever

Herbal tea helps to combat fever. Try equal parts of peppermint, yarrow and elderflower. Drink the tea as hot as possible, go to bed and sweat. Lemongrass tea is also good for feverish colds.

Eat Less

When you're ill, your appetite will tend to be poor. This is because your body needs to spend its energy on repairing itself rather than digesting food. A good rule: when ill, eat lightly, if at all, and try to eat more raw foods. A better rule: fasting will fix you faster.

Drink lots of water as well as fruit and vegetable juices. You can get the minerals and vitamins you need in supplement (tablet) form while you give your body a short metabolic holiday.

1. Body-building Exercises

First, let's get the cheap excuses out of the way:

- I'm too poor to join a gym.
  You don't have to.
- I can't even afford to buy equipment and work out at home.
  You don't have to.
- I get bored doing exercises.
  Forget a career in performance.

And with these exercises, singers lose their favourite excuse for not practising— I can't make much noise where I live. These exercises are all gloriously silent!

EXERCISES FOR THE DEEPER THORACIC MUSCULATURE

1. Isometric

- Stand in a doorway and exert pressure outwards onto the architrave with both hands. Breathing unregulated.
- Face the architrave of a doorway and exert pressure on the wall from either side, as if you were trying to squeeze the wall from either side. Breathing unregulated.
- Face one side of a doorway, cross your arms, and then exert pressure on the wall from either side, as if you were trying to wrench the wall apart, using your hands. Breathing unregulated.

2. Lying down

- Get a dumb-bell or a brick in a sock. Lie on your back on a flat surface with your arms above your head and the brick or dumb-bell held in both hands. Raise your arms above your head, while you *breathe out*. Return arms to behind your head (floor level), while you *breathe in*.
- Get two dumb-bells or bricks in socks. Lie on your stomah on a narrow kitchen table or a narrow futon (not a bouncy bed.) Your body should be fully supported by the table or the futon; only your head should extend over the end. Holding a brick/dumb-bell in each hand, let your arms dangle down over each side of the table/futon. Raise your arms like a bird, up as far as

possible, while you *breathe out*. When your arms are at the highest point of their movement, *breathe in*. Lower your arms on a *held breath*.

AN EXERCISE FOR THE CHEST AND BACK
(ROSES AND ROPES)

I'm indebted to Irwin K. Kellog for one of the most universally useful toning-up exercises for singing performers that I've ever come across. His book of illustrated breathing exercise, first published in 1927, is deliciously titled *Why Breathe?* Here is his description of the exercise precisely as Irwin tells it:

> FOR RAISING THE CHEST AND STRENGTHENING THE BACK
> Stand erect with weight on the balls of the feet. To secure this balance, raise the heels from the floor, and stand tiptoe, first on both feet, then on one. Lower the heels to the floor, but do not let the weight rest upon them. Draw the abdomen inward, by making a straight, instead of an inward-curved line at the small of the back. If the fleshy part of the back is curved inward and down, it will draw the abdomen into proper position. The weak muscles of the abdomen should be tensed and strengthened, so they will retain correct position without support. Think of drawing the lower part of the shoulder blades almost together. This narrows the back, raises the flat breast bone, and lengthens the line from neck to waist. "Wear your chest in front, not in the back."
> A ball rolled from the breast bone should not touch anything until it reaches the tip of the foot. This position throws the organs of the body into proper balance. It enables the diaphragm to work freely, and gives what is known as "relaxed breathing" ...
> Dropping the arms at full length in front of the body, place the backs of the hands together. Inhale through nose as though smelling the perfume of a flower as you bring the arms upward, hands touching the body ... from waist to chest, nose and top of head. Separating the hands, stretch the arms upward as straight as possible. Hold the breath easily until the end of the exercise.
> Lower the arms to shoulder height; at this point imagine that a rope is stretched from floor to ceiling at either side, which can be grasped firmly in the clenched fist, and pulled inward. This is to give a strong counteraction to expanding the chest. Bend the arm at the elbow, bringing in the hands to the raised chest at shoulder height. Exhale and relax.
>
> Irwin K. Kellogg, Why Breathe?, edn no. 413,
Allans, Melbourne, 1927

Here, lacking Irwin's eloquence, is my boiled-down summary of 'Roses and Ropes':

• Stand straight, with body weight on your toes.
• Bottom in and down.
• Bring base of shoulder blades together.

- Arms down in front of your body; backs of your hands together.
- Breathe in through your nose as if smelling a rose.
- At the same time, smoothly bring your hands together upwards, touching the front of your body.
- When you've breathed in fully, your hands will be stretched straight above your head.
- Now, while holding that breath, imagine two steel ropes strung from floor to ceiling, one on each side of you.
- Reach out aSs far as you can, with arms at shoulder level, and grasp the ropes.
- Slowly, and against huge resistance, stretch the two ropes until you have brought them to touch in the centre of your chest.
- Breathe out now and relax. You'll need to.

2. Cool-down Exercises

When the show's over, you haven't quite finished your day's work. Athletes habitually do cool-down exercises after activity in order to ease their bodies back down to an everyday functional level. It makes equal sense to give yourself a smooth transition between the extraordinary emotional and physical demands of performance and the less heightened state of ordinary, day-to-day life. Why cool-downs? They minimise the likelihood of muscles becoming 'fixed' during high-energy activity: a role you perform for a year can 'fix' your musculature in ways that may make it difficult for you to tackle other genres and styles in the future. In addition, cool-downs help to maintain vocal flexibility by reducing muscle tissue temperature, preventing blood pooling, and therefore allowing blood to lactic acid from muscles.

Mark Meylan, a fine British teacher and coach who works with many music theatre performers, is one of many advocates for the regular use of cool-down exercises for performers. Suggesting that it should become a post-show habit, Meylan cheerfully calls it 'putting your toys away after playing with them'.

If you think of a cool-down as a warm-up backwards, you will know what to do to return your voice and body from 'stage speed' to 'street speed'. Everything should be done gently, easily and quietly, and should never last longer than ten minutes.

In addition, Meylan suggests a simple five minute cool-down for mid-performance intervals. As soon as you come off stage, sustain a comfortable, low hum for a minute. Follow this with a minute's silence, then a minute more of hum, then another minute's silence, then finish with another minute of gentle, low humming.

Bibliography

BAXTER, Mark, *The Rock-n-Roll Singer's Survival Manual,* Hal Leonard Publishing, Milwaukee, 1989.

CALLAGHAN, J., *Singing and Voice Science,* Singular Press, San Diego, 2000.

CHENG, Stephen Chun-Tao, *The Tao of Voice: A New East-West Approach to Transforming the Singing and Speaking Voice,* Destiny Books, Rochester (Vt), Destiny Books, 1991.

CRAIG, David, *A Performer Prepares: a Guide to Song Preparation for Actors, Singers and Dancers,* Applause, New York, 1993.

CRAIG, David, *On Singing Onstage,* 2nd edn, Applause, New York, 2990.

EDGLEY, Jeni, *Jeni Edgley's Nutrition Book,* Lansdowne, Sydney, 1985.

FOSTER, Roland, *Vocal Success and How to Achieve It,* orig. edn., W.H. Paling, Sydney, 1935, reprinted by Chappell Music, Sydney, n.d.

KELLOGG, Irwin K., *Why Breathe?,* Allans, Melbourne, edn. no. 413, 1927.

LAINE, Cleo, *You Can Sing If You Want To,* Victor Gollancz, London,1997.

SALAMAN, Esther, *Unlocking Your Voice: Freedom to Sing,* Victor Gollancz, London 1996.

SATALOFF, Robert Thayer, *Professional Voice: The Science and Art of Clinical Care,* Raven, New York, 1991.

Index